GCSE English

A Christmas Carol

by Charles Dickens

A Christmas Carol... it's definitely a classic bit of Dickens.
But writing essays about it? That can be a challenge.

Not to worry. This brilliant Text Guide explains the whole novel —
characters, language, themes, historical background... the lot. And because
it's a CGP book, we get straight to the point, with no needless rambling.

We've also included plenty of practice questions to test you on what you've learned,
plus a whole section of advice on how to plan and write brilliant
answers in the exams. It's a bargain, even by Scrooge's standards!

The Text Guide

CONTENTS

Contents

Published by CGP

Editors:
David Broadbent
Emma Crighton
Anna Hall

Contributor:
Nicola Woodfin

With thanks to Heather Gregson and Paula Barnett for the proofreading,
and Jan Greenway for the copyright research.

Acknowledgements:

Cover Illustration and image on page 4 ~ A Christmas Carol (detail) © Dean Morrissey, licensed by The Greenwich Workshop, Inc. www.greenwichworkshop.com

With thanks to Rex Features for permission to use the images on pages 3, 4, 5, 13, 17, 24, 25, 30, 31, 33, 37, 38, 39, 40, 41, 42, 43, 49 & 52

With thanks to iStockphoto.com for permission to use the images on pages 1, 2, 3 & 32

With thanks to Mary Evans Picture Library for permission to use the images on pages 1, 6, 7, 8 & 9

With thanks to Kobal for permission to use the images on pages 16, 46, 48 & 51

With thanks to ArenaPAL.com for permission to use the images on pages 3, 4, 5, 12, 14, 15, 18, 19, 20, 21, 26, 27, 28, 29, 36, 47 & 50

ISBN: 978 1 78294 309 9
Printed by Elanders Ltd, Newcastle upon Tyne.
Clipart from Corel®

Based on the classic CGP style created by Richard Parsons.

Introducing 'A Christmas Carol' and Dickens

'A Christmas Carol' is about a miser called Scrooge

- *A Christmas Carol* is a short novel (or <u>novella</u>) about a bitter <u>miser</u> called Scrooge. With the help of three <u>ghosts</u>, Scrooge <u>changes</u> dramatically, and becomes <u>kind</u> and <u>generous</u> by the end of the book.

- Although it's a <u>fictional</u> story, the novel explores the very <u>real</u> problem of <u>poverty</u> in Victorian society. It <u>criticises</u> the attitudes of many rich people, who Dickens saw as dismissing and ignoring the problem.

A Christmas Carol has a strong message

1) *A Christmas Carol* strongly emphasises the importance of <u>social responsibility</u> — Dickens argues in the novel that people have a <u>duty</u> to help the <u>less fortunate</u>.

2) The novel is set at <u>Christmas</u>. Dickens saw Christmas as a <u>special</u> time of year, when people treated each other with kindness and generosity. This was an attitude that he believed should continue <u>all year round</u>.

A nineteenth-century slum in London

© iStockphoto.com/duncan1890

Charles Dickens experienced poverty as a child

- Dickens's family was <u>middle-class</u>, but he knew what it was like to be <u>poor</u>. When Dickens was twelve, his father was <u>imprisoned</u> for debt. The family was very poor, so Dickens had to work in a <u>factory</u>.

- Dickens's experience of <u>poverty</u> made him <u>critical</u> of the way Victorian society treated its <u>poorest people</u>.

1812	<u>Born</u> on 7th February, in <u>Portsmouth</u>.
1824	His father is <u>arrested for debt</u> and sent to <u>prison</u>. Dickens has to give up his education and work in a factory.
1824-27	His father <u>inherits</u> some money so Dickens goes to <u>private school</u> for two years.
1827	Works as an office boy at a <u>solicitor's firm</u>.
1828	Starts work as a <u>court reporter</u>.
1833	<u>First short story</u> published — 'A Dinner at Poplar Walk'.
1836	<u>Marries</u> Catherine Hogarth.
1836-37	His first novel '<u>Pickwick Papers</u>' is serialised.
1843	'A Christmas Carol' is published.
1870	<u>Dies</u> of a stroke on 9th June. Buried in <u>Westminster Abbey</u>.

© Mary Evans Picture Library

Background Information

'A Christmas Carol' is set in London

Here's a <u>map</u> of the main locations in the novel:

The Cratchits' House

Fred's House

Scrooge's Office

Scrooge's House

London

Dickens thought that the rich should help the poor

1) <u>Poverty</u> was a huge <u>problem</u> in Victorian society, particularly in over-crowded <u>cities</u> like London.

2) Dickens was very <u>concerned</u> by this — his own <u>experiences</u> with poverty had taught him how unpleasant it could be.

3) He strongly believed that it was the <u>responsibility</u> of the wealthy to <u>help</u> those who were in poverty. He believed that ignoring this responsibility would eventually cause much <u>bigger problems</u>.

4) Dickens urged people to <u>help</u> the poor by providing them with <u>education</u> and by donating to, and working with, <u>charities</u>.

A Victorian soup kitchen

Introduction

Who's Who in 'A Christmas Carol'

Ebenezer Scrooge...

...is a miserly, bitter old man, who has no friends and hates Christmas. He's the main character in the book.

© Ray Tang/REX

© REX

Marley's ghost...

...is the spirit of Scrooge's old business partner, Jacob Marley. Like Scrooge, he spent his life alone.

© Michael Le Poer Trench/ArenaPAL

Ghost of Christmas Past...

...is both childlike and aged in appearance. It shows Scrooge scenes from his past.

Ghost of Christmas Present...

...is a giant, jolly spirit, who shows Scrooge how other people celebrate Christmas.

© KINGWILL Marilyn/ ArenaPAL

Ghost of Christmas Yet to Come...

...is a silent, hooded figure. It shows Scrooge what will happen after he dies.

© iStockphoto.com/Bliznetsov

© Moviestore Collection/REX

Bob Cratchit...

...is Scrooge's employee. He's a good person who loves his family. He doesn't have much money.

© iStockphoto.com/kparis

Fred...

...is Scrooge's nephew. He's a cheerful man, who's very generous, and always friendly to his uncle.

Tiny Tim...

...is Bob's son. He's ill and walks with a crutch. He's selfless and well-loved by those around him.

© Ray Tang/REX

Introduction

'A Christmas Carol' — Plot Summary

'A Christmas Carol'... what happens when?

Here's a quick round-up of everything that happens in *A Christmas Carol*. It's no substitute for actually reading the book, but these pages should help you remember it all better when you get to your exam.

Chapter One — Scrooge receives a warning

- Ebenezer Scrooge is in his <u>counting-house</u>. It's Christmas Eve and both he and his clerk, Bob Cratchit, are still working.

- Fred, Scrooge's nephew, arrives to wish his uncle a Merry Christmas, and to <u>invite</u> him to celebrate with his family. Scrooge rudely refuses his offer.

- Scrooge arrives <u>home</u>, and as he's about to open his door he sees the <u>face</u> of Jacob Marley (his old business partner) in the <u>door knocker</u>.

- Later that evening, Marley's <u>ghost</u> appears in Scrooge's bedroom. Marley is wrapped in a heavy chain and <u>doomed</u> to endlessly roam the earth.

- Marley says that Scrooge will suffer the <u>same</u> fate as him unless he <u>changes</u> his ways. He explains that Scrooge will be visited by <u>three spirits</u> and that they're his <u>only chance</u> of saving himself.

Chapter Two — the first ghost shows Scrooge his past

- The <u>Ghost of Christmas Past</u> appears to Scrooge.

- The ghost takes Scrooge to the <u>village</u> where he grew up, and Scrooge sees his younger self at <u>school</u>, where he's spending Christmas <u>alone</u>.

- Scrooge then sees some happier Christmases: his <u>sister</u> Fan coming to take him home from school, and a <u>party</u> organised by his old <u>boss</u>, Mr Fezziwig.

- Next, Scrooge is taken to see the moment when his <u>fiancée</u>, Belle, broke off their <u>engagement</u> because of Scrooge's obsession with money.

- He then sees Belle <u>grown up</u>, with a family of her own.

- Scrooge <u>struggles</u> with the ghost to make it <u>stop</u> the visions and he's transported back to his bedroom.

Chapter Three — Scrooge learns about the joy of Christmas

- The Ghost of Christmas Present arrives. It's jolly and friendly.

- Scrooge and the ghost visit Bob Cratchit's family, who are enjoying their Christmas Day. Scrooge learns that Bob's son, Tiny Tim, will die in the near future.

- Scrooge and the ghost travel the world, visiting other people. They're all enjoying Christmas.

- They then visit Fred's house. The people there make fun of Scrooge and his attitude towards Christmas.

- The ghost reveals two starving children hidden within its robes. The children are named Ignorance and Want — the ghost warns Scrooge to beware of them.

Chapter Four — Scrooge sees his future

- The Ghost of Christmas Yet to Come comes to collect Scrooge.

- The ghost silently shows Scrooge the reaction of some people to the death of an unknown man. Nobody seems to care very much that the man is dead.

- An undertaker, a charwoman (cleaner) and a laundress try to sell the dead man's belongings, which they've stolen. They've even taken the shirt from his body.

- Scrooge and the ghost visit Bob Cratchit's family. Scrooge discovers Tiny Tim has died, and the Cratchits are very upset.

- The ghost takes Scrooge to a graveyard, and points to a grave with Scrooge's name on it. Scrooge promises to the ghost that he will honour Christmas and change the course of his life.

Chapter Five — Scrooge is a changed man

- Scrooge finds himself back in his own bed. He discovers that it's still Christmas Day.

- Scrooge has completely changed — he laughs and wishes passers-by a Merry Christmas. He buys the Cratchit family a huge turkey, then joins Fred and his companions for Christmas dinner. The next day, Scrooge gives Bob a pay rise.

- We're told that Tiny Tim will survive, and that Scrooge celebrates Christmas for the rest of his life.

'A Christmas Carol' — not a lot of actual carol-singing...

A Christmas Carol isn't a particularly long novel, but it packs a punch — it gets critical about lots of gritty social issues, as well as injecting a bit of bonus Christmas spirit into things. If you're happy with the plot, have a look at Section One for some background info. If not, try having a gander at the cartoon at the back of the book.

Section One — Background and Context

Poverty in Victorian Britain

Poverty was a huge problem in Dickens's time. Originally, he wanted to write a pamphlet to raise awareness about poverty, but he decided that a short Christmas story would spread the message more effectively.

The Industrial Revolution created lots of jobs

1) From <u>1780</u>, factory owners in Britain began to use coal-fired <u>steam engines</u> to power the machines in big factories. Many of these factories made <u>cloth</u>, which was sold all around the world.

2) Before this, Britain used to be much more <u>rural</u> — <u>farming</u> was the most obvious way of making a living.

3) This period — where most people in Britain went from working in farming to working in manufacturing — was known as the <u>Industrial Revolution</u>.

> **Character — Scrooge**
>
> At the start of *A Christmas Carol*, <u>Ebenezer Scrooge</u> is presented as a <u>wealthy</u> man who ignores the <u>poverty</u> around him, including that of Bob Cratchit, his employee.

4) The Industrial Revolution made many businessmen and factory owners extremely <u>rich</u>. It also created huge numbers of new <u>jobs</u> in the cities. However, the factory workers often lived in extreme <u>poverty</u>.

Many cities had terrible living conditions

1) In the nineteenth century, millions of people moved from the countryside to the <u>cities</u> in search of <u>work</u> in the factories. As a result, the <u>population</u> of cities grew rapidly — between 1800 and 1900, London's population <u>grew</u> from roughly 1 million people to 6 million.

© Illustrated London News Ltd/Mary Evans

2) Most of these migrants ended up living in <u>slums</u> of cheap, overcrowded housing. There was often no proper drainage or <u>sewage</u> systems, and many families were forced to share one tap and toilet. Overcrowding led to <u>hunger</u>, <u>disease</u> and <u>crime</u>.

3) <u>Children</u> often suffered the most from these conditions — they were <u>exploited</u> by wealthy factory owners and forced to work long hours in dangerous conditions.

> Dickens was very interested in the plight of the <u>poor</u> due to his own <u>childhood</u> experience of <u>poverty</u> when his family went into <u>debt</u>. Dickens had to work in a blacking factory (where black dye for boots was made) to help pay off those debts. He wrote several <u>novels</u> and <u>articles</u> addressing poverty in Britain — e.g. *Hard Times* and *Oliver Twist*.

Poverty in 'A Christmas Carol'

Dickens uses *A Christmas Carol* to highlight the <u>poverty</u> of working-class London.

- He <u>contrasts</u> the wealth of Scrooge with the poverty of Bob Cratchit. Scrooge lives alone in a <u>large</u> building with a grand staircase, while the Cratchits are <u>crammed</u> into a four-roomed house in the suburbs.

- In Chapter Four, Scrooge visits a part of London that "<u>reeked</u> with <u>crime</u>, with <u>filth</u>, and <u>misery</u>", and the people who live there are described as "half-naked, drunken, slipshod, ugly".

- The <u>death</u> of Tiny Tim, and the appearance of the <u>doomed</u> children, Ignorance and Want, highlight the suffering of <u>children</u> who live in poverty.

You've got to think about the context of the text...

Authors don't write their books in a dark room shut off from the world. They're influenced by the important issues and events of their time. To make sense of a text you need to be aware of some of these things.

Malthus and the 1834 Poor Law

So I'm sure you've worked out by now that poverty was a big problem in Victorian society. As with any problem, people disagreed about the best way to find a solution. Some thought poverty was just inevitable...

Malthus argued that poverty was inevitable

1) In 1798, the economist Thomas Malthus wrote that the human <u>population</u> would always grow faster than <u>food supplies</u>. This would mean that <u>overpopulation</u> would lead to many people, usually the poor, <u>dying</u> due to famine. For Malthus, poverty was the <u>inevitable</u> result of overpopulation because the worst-off in society would get less and less.

2) Malthus argued that people should have families <u>later</u> in life and not have lots of <u>children</u> to stop the population getting too <u>large</u>.

3) Dickens believed that Malthus was <u>wrong</u> and that there was plenty of food to go around — but only if the <u>rich</u> were more <u>generous</u>. He thought it was wrong that the poor should <u>suffer</u> because the rich were too <u>selfish</u> to share their wealth.

Thomas Robert Malthus

4) In Chapter Three, the Ghost of Christmas Present takes Scrooge to <u>bustling</u> shops where it shows him the <u>huge amount</u> of food on display. This lengthy, mouth-watering description emphasises Dickens's point that there was <u>plenty</u> of food to go around — the problem was that it wasn't <u>shared</u> with the poor.

> In Chapter One, <u>Scrooge</u> tells the charity collectors that it would be better if <u>poor</u> people would <u>die</u> and in doing so "decrease the <u>surplus population</u>". This is a direct reference to Malthus's theories — Dickens is highlighting how <u>cruel</u> Malthus's views seemed to be.

Some people thought helping the poor made poverty worse

1) Malthus, and others, thought that the existing <u>poor laws</u> in Britain were too <u>charitable</u> — they argued that poverty relief for the poor encouraged <u>laziness</u> and reduced the incentive to work hard and save money.

2) In <u>1834</u> a new <u>Poor Law</u> was introduced to <u>reduce</u> the financial help available to the poor. It ruled that all unemployed people would have to enter a <u>workhouse</u> in order to receive food and shelter.

3) However, these workhouses were extremely <u>harsh</u> places — inhabitants had to work hard and families were often split up. Many people lived in <u>fear</u> of being forced to enter a workhouse, where the conditions were made deliberately unpleasant to <u>discourage</u> the poor from relying on society to help them.

4) In *A Christmas Carol*, Dickens attacks what he saw as an <u>uncaring</u> attitude towards the poor. In Chapter One, Scrooge tells the charity collectors that he can't afford to "make <u>idle</u> people merry", and he says that he <u>supports</u> the prisons and workhouses. His views seem cruel and unfeeling.

5) When Scrooge expresses <u>sympathy</u> for Tiny Tim and Ignorance and Want, the spirit <u>quotes</u> Scrooge's harsh comments from Chapter One about "<u>surplus population</u>" and sending the poor to <u>prisons</u> and <u>workhouses</u>. Scrooge realises that his beliefs about the poor were <u>wrong</u>.

KEY QUOTE

"If they would rather die... they had better do it"

It was no good handing out cash, if all it did was encourage people to be lazy. But then again, waiting for the poor to die and thereby decrease the surplus population doesn't exactly sound kind. Hmmm...

Charity and Education

Dickens wasn't such a fan of the idea of 'surplus population' — he was frustrated with those who dismissed poverty as inevitable. He thought the rich should try harder to help the poor to improve their lives.

Dickens highlighted the importance of generosity and charity

1) The Industrial Revolution created a society in which the gap between the rich and poor was huge. Many of those struggling to survive in extreme poverty relied on the generosity of those better off than themselves.

2) For example, some very successful philanthropist businessmen were keen to enhance the lives of their workers. The famous chocolate makers, the Cadburys, tried to provide quality homes and improve lifestyles for workers at their factory in Bournville, near Birmingham. Titus Salt, a cloth maker, did a similar thing in Saltaire in Yorkshire.

   A philanthropist is someone who tries to help other people by performing charitable acts.

3) However, many other wealthy people were only concerned with gaining more wealth — like Scrooge. Dickens attacked this kind of selfishness — he believed that wealthy people had a responsibility to help those less fortunate than themselves.

Scrooge Learns the Value of Charity

- In Chapter One, Marley's ghost warns Scrooge that he must pay more attention to those around him. He can't walk among "crowds of fellow-beings" with his "eyes turned down" like Marley did.

- By the end of the novel, Scrooge has learned his lesson and changed his attitude towards charity — he gives a large sum of money to the charity collectors.

- Scrooge also learns to generously reward other people's work — he gives Bob Cratchit a pay rise and pays a boy a large fee to run and fetch the prize turkey from the Poulterer's. Dickens uses Scrooge's actions to suggest that if people were paid fairly, there would be less need for charity.

Dickens believed education was the solution to poverty

1) Dickens believed that many of the problems in Victorian society — such as crime, poverty and disease — were caused by a lack of education. The poor in Victorian Britain had little or no education, and Dickens felt that education would help them to gain self-respect and improve their lives.

2) Dickens supported several projects to educate the poor, such as the Ragged Schools, which offered free education, clothing and food to children from poor families — they were called 'ragged' after the ragged clothes the children wore.

3) In Chapter Three of *A Christmas Carol*, Dickens uses the child, Ignorance, to show how the poor are doomed to a life of want by a lack of education. The Ghost of Christmas Present suggests that without education, those who live in ignorance and want have no refuge except prisons and workhouses.

A 'Ragged School'

© Illustrated London News Ltd/Mary Evans

EXAM TIP

Show how Dickens's views come through in the novel...

Knowing Dickens's ideas on charity and education should help you to get a better grasp of his message in the novel. He wanted to find practical ways to help the poor. What a lovely bloke he was.

Religion and Christmas

It's important to understand Dickens's views on Christianity. His idea of a good Christian was someone who did their best to help other people. You'll notice this idea coming up a few times in the novel...

Victorian society was very religious

A family Bible reading

1) Christianity had a strong influence on many areas of everyday life in Victorian Britain, particularly amongst the middle and upper classes. To be good Christians, people believed they should live by a strict moral code — attending church regularly, avoiding alcohol and exercising sexual restraint.

2) Dickens's view of Christianity was different — he believed that to be a good Christian, people should seek out opportunities to do good deeds for other people. He thought that people should be humble, charitable, faithful and forgiving, rather than merely appearing religious.

3) It was a widespread Victorian practice to spend Sunday going to church and resting — this was known as Sabbatarianism. Dickens was opposed to this (he was an anti-Sabbatarian) because it meant that working poorer people were denied any enjoyment on their one day off — everything was shut.

4) Many poorer people didn't have ovens at home, so they often had their food cooked by bakers. Sabbatarianism meant that many people couldn't get a hot meal on Sundays because the bakers were shut.

5) In Chapter Three, Scrooge complains to the Ghost of Christmas Present that keeping Sunday as a day of rest denies the poor of "opportunities of innocent enjoyment" on the only day when they don't have to work, and it will "deprive" them of a cooked dinner.

Christmas became more important

1) At the start of the nineteenth century, Christmas was hardly celebrated at all. However, by the end of the century, it had become the most important celebration of the year.

2) Many traditions that are associated with Christmas became increasingly important, such as cards, crackers, carols, decorations, gifts and Christmas dinner.

3) Christmas celebrations were becoming more secular, too, as feasts and games became a central part of the festivities. In the novel, both Fred and Fezziwig host Christmas parties full of fun, dancing, laughter and food.

If something is 'secular', it's not connected with religion.

Theme — The Christmas Spirit

A Christmas Carol focuses on charity, forgiveness, goodwill and generosity — values which are an important part of the spirit of Christmas, and also reflect Dickens's view of Christianity. A key message in the novel is that people should try to observe these values all year round, not just at Christmas — Scrooge promises, "I will honour Christmas in my heart, and try to keep it all the year".

KEY QUOTE

"a kind, forgiving, charitable, pleasant time"

The important thing to pick out here is the focus on family and Christmas spirit, and how all that Christmas cheer could continue throughout the year. Think about how this relates to Dickens's view of Christianity.

Section One — Background and Context

Practice Questions

The clue's in the title — yep, you guessed it, they're questions to help you to practise for the exam. This page is full of quick questions to check you've remembered everything from the section. You only need to write a few words for each, so it shouldn't take too long. If there's anything you can't get on the first go, take a look back at the section, and then have another go. Think of it like a quiz. Unfortunately there are no prizes... just pride.

Quick Questions

1) Which of the following sentences is correct?
   a) The Industrial Revolution led to more people working in farming.
   b) The Industrial Revolution led to more people working in manufacturing.

2) What happened to the population of many British cities in the nineteenth century?

3) What happened during Dickens's childhood that made him interested in the plight of poor people?

4) Who was Thomas Malthus?

5) What did Malthus think people should do to avoid overpopulation in society?

6) Why were workhouses made deliberately unpleasant?

7) The Industrial Revolution narrowed the gap between the rich and the poor. True or false?

8) What is a 'philanthropist'?

9) Why did Dickens think education was important?

Practice Questions

Lucky you — more practice questions. But I've spiced things up a bit this time. You've got a few more quick questions and then some meaty, in-depth questions to sink your teeth into. These should take a bit longer than the quick questions. There's no need to write a whole essay though — a paragraph will do. The important thing is for you to get to grips with the context of the novel.

Quick Questions

10) What is the name given to the schools for the poor that Dickens supported?

11) What is Sabbatarianism?

12) Christmas celebrations became more secular in the nineteenth century. True or false?

13) List three Christmas traditions that were part of Victorian Christmas celebrations.

In-depth Questions

1) Explain two effects of the Industrial Revolution on British society.

2) Briefly explain Malthus's theory on overpopulation and how overpopulation can affect the poor.

3) Do you think Dickens agreed or disagreed with the workhouses?
   Use quotes from the novel to support your answer.

4) Does Dickens present Sabbatarianism in a positive way?
   Use evidence from the text in your answer.

5) What evidence is there in the text that Christmas was not just a
   religious celebration at the time when Dickens was writing?

Chapter Analysis — Marley's Ghost

This section takes a closer look at everything that happens in *A Christmas Carol*. The first chapter starts by introducing us to Scrooge — oh, and we also get to meet our first ghost...

The narrator introduces Scrooge

Omniscient narrators aren't part of the action, but know everything that happens.

1) The chapter begins <u>lightheartedly</u> as the <u>omniscient narrator</u> humorously discusses the fact that Jacob Marley is dead.

2) However, the chapter becomes less lighthearted when Scrooge, Marley's old <u>business partner</u>, is introduced. He's mean, greedy and "solitary as an oyster". His "shrivelled" looks and "grating voice" match his horrible personality.

3) The cheerful beginning of the novel <u>contrasts</u> with Scrooge's introduction — it makes Scrooge seem <u>even less appealing</u>.

Writer's Techniques

The <u>narrator</u> uses the phrase "Once upon a time" to <u>introduce</u> the main story. Dickens's use of a <u>fairy tale convention</u> suggests that the story will have a <u>magical</u> element to it and that it's likely to have a <u>happy ending</u>.

© Nigel Norrington / ArenaPAL

Scrooge is rude to everyone

1) Scrooge's office is dark and cold. He's too <u>mean</u> to let his clerk, Bob Cratchit, have a decent fire.

2) Scrooge's <u>nephew</u> Fred arrives to wish him a Merry Christmas. Fred is Scrooge's <u>opposite</u> — Scrooge is <u>cynical</u> and <u>negative</u> about Christmas, but Fred thinks Christmas is "a kind, forgiving, charitable, pleasant time". Scrooge says that everybody who wishes others Merry Christmas is an "<u>idiot</u>".

3) Scrooge's <u>nasty personality</u> is developed by his treatment of the charity collectors, who come to his office looking for donations. He <u>refuses</u> to donate money, saying that the poor are "<u>idle</u>".

4) Later, a <u>boy</u> starts to sing a <u>Christmas carol</u> through Scrooge's keyhole, but Scrooge <u>scares</u> him so much that he flees "in terror". Scrooge is then <u>rude</u> to Bob when he reluctantly allows him to spend Christmas Day with his family instead of at work.

Theme — Social Responsibility

Scrooge represents <u>selfish</u> members of the middle and upper classes in Victorian society. He <u>refuses</u> to give to charity, and he calls poor people "surplus population", saying it would be better if they <u>died</u>.

Character — Scrooge

Scrooge is <u>difficult</u> and <u>unpleasant</u> to everybody he comes into contact with at the start of the book. Dickens establishes Scrooge as an <u>unsympathetic</u> figure to make his transformation more <u>powerful</u>.

Dickens links Scrooge with the weather

1) The weather in this chapter is "bleak" and <u>ominous</u> — it seems like nature "was brewing on a large scale". This creates the impression that something <u>big</u> is about to happen.

2) Dickens often links the weather with Scrooge's <u>personality</u> — here it's <u>cold</u>, which reflects the "cold within" Scrooge's heart. It's also <u>foggy</u>, which could symbolise Scrooge's inability to see how <u>ignorant</u> he's being. The weather gets <u>worse</u> during the chapter as more of Scrooge's unpleasant <u>personality</u> is revealed.

3) These bleak conditions suggests that there's something <u>unsettling</u> about Scrooge's behaviour.

Chapter Analysis — Marley's Ghost

Scrooge's house is dreary and dark

1) Scrooge returns to his <u>rooms</u>, which used to belong to Marley. They're <u>dark</u>, because "darkness is cheap" — they reflect Scrooge's cold and miserly personality.

2) As he's about to enter, Scrooge's door knocker <u>transforms</u> into Marley's face. This is the first glimpse of the <u>supernatural</u> in the novel, and it <u>foreshadows</u> the ghostly visitations that follow.

Foreshadowing is a technique used by writers to hint at something that will happen later in the story.

3) The dramatic tension <u>rises</u> as more <u>strange</u> things start to occur — Scrooge sees Marley's <u>face</u> in the tiles of his fireplace, all the <u>bells</u> in the house start to ring, and he hears the clanking of <u>chains</u> from the cellar.

Marley's ghost comes to haunt Scrooge

KEY EVENT

© Ray Tang/REX

1) Marley's ghost appears, wearing a heavy <u>chain</u> of "cash-boxes, keys, padlocks, ledgers, deeds and heavy purses". These items symbolise how Marley was <u>obsessed</u> with <u>money</u> — just like Scrooge.

2) Marley's obsession with money led to his lack of <u>compassion</u> and <u>care</u> for others. As a result, Marley is "<u>doomed</u> to wander through the world" forever, and he refers to his fate as an "incessant <u>torture</u>".

3) Marley suggests that Scrooge is <u>worse</u> than him — Scrooge's chain was as <u>heavy</u> as Marley's "seven Christmas Eves ago". Dickens implies that Scrooge might be in for an even <u>more horrible</u> fate than Marley.

4) Scrooge finds out that he'll have one last chance at <u>redemption</u> — he'll be visited by <u>three ghosts</u> over the course of the next three nights.

Scrooge experiences unfamiliar emotions

This chapter is the <u>beginning</u> of Scrooge's <u>transformation</u> — he's starting to experience <u>new</u> emotions:

- The appearance of Marley's face in his door knocker gives Scrooge a "<u>terrible sensation</u>" he hasn't felt since "infancy". He hasn't been this <u>afraid</u> since he was a <u>child</u>.

- When he sees Marley's ghost, he has to make <u>jokes</u> to try to keep "down his <u>terror</u>" — despite being "not much in the habit" of trying to be funny. This emphasises just how frightened he is.

- He <u>begs</u> for some explanation or comfort from Marley's ghost, speaking with "<u>humility</u> and <u>deference</u>". This contrasts with the way he speaks <u>earlier</u> in the chapter.

- He <u>tries</u> to say "humbug" about the warning from Marley, but he can't finish the word — this is a sign that he's <u>already changing</u> and losing his <u>negative</u> outlook on life.

KEY QUOTE

"Humbug, I tell you — humbug!"

Maybe we should bring back some Victorian slang. Humbug's a useful phrase when your teachers try to tell you off for forgetting your homework. Or for when the ghost of your old business partner turns up.

Chapter Analysis — The First of the Three Spirits

In this chapter, Scrooge is taught the first of his big ghostly lessons — the Ghost of Christmas Past takes him to see a load of scenes from his life. Turns out Scrooge wasn't always such a grump — who knew, eh?

The Ghost of Christmas Past appears to Scrooge

1) The first spirit appears as the clock strikes one — even though Scrooge had fallen asleep after two. The time is completely <u>impossible</u> — so the chapter feels <u>magical</u>.

2) The spirit tells Scrooge that it's the spirit of Scrooge's <u>own past</u> — and it claims to be there to <u>help</u> him.

3) Scrooge wants the spirit to put its <u>cap</u> on, to <u>hide</u> the light that shines from its head. This could suggest that Scrooge is <u>reluctant</u> to face up to the truth of his past actions. The spirit also implies that Scrooge's mean and miserly <u>attitude</u> has helped to <u>create</u> the cap that suppresses its light.

> **Writer's Techniques**
>
> The striking clock is <u>repeated</u> throughout the story, to show that time has passed, and that a <u>new section</u> in the book is beginning. The clock also adds <u>suspense</u> to this chapter, as Scrooge is left counting down until the ghost appears.

Scrooge reacts emotionally to the visions

© Nigel Norrington / ArenaPAL

1) When Scrooge sees his past, he acts <u>completely differently</u> to how he behaves in Chapter One — when the people from his old <u>village</u> wish each other Merry Christmas, it fills him with "gladness".

2) Seeing his old school has a "<u>softening</u> influence" on Scrooge. This contrasts with the earlier description of him as "Hard and sharp".

3) Scrooge sobs with pity when he sees himself in a lonely <u>schoolroom</u>. The feeling makes him <u>regret</u> scaring away the carol singer in Chapter One — he's learning to <u>empathise</u> with other people.

4) However, this is a <u>happy</u> memory for Scrooge as well as a sad one — the young Scrooge is kept company by the characters from the <u>books</u> he's reading. This shows us Scrooge's <u>imaginative</u> side.

> **Theme — The Christmas Spirit**
>
> This is the <u>first point</u> in the novel when Scrooge reacts <u>positively</u> to the mention of Christmas. This suggests that Christmas was once <u>important</u> to him.

Scrooge loved his sister

1) In the next vision, Scrooge's <u>sister</u>, Fan, says that their father has <u>changed</u> and is "much kinder" now — Scrooge will be allowed to come home from school, and they'll be <u>together</u> for Christmas.

2) The <u>transformation</u> of Scrooge's father <u>foreshadows</u> Scrooge's own transformation, and suggests that his change will also positively <u>affect</u> the people around him.

3) Scrooge is reminded of his sister's "large heart". We learn that Fan is dead and that Fred is the son of the sister Scrooge <u>loved</u>. This forces Scrooge to <u>reconsider</u> his relationship with Fred — he feels "<u>uneasy</u> in his mind" about the way he's <u>treated</u> him.

> **Writer's Techniques**
>
> Dickens uses the <u>five senses</u> to make Scrooge's past seem more <u>vivid</u>. For example, he mentions the "cheerful voices" and music of Fezziwig's party, and the "thousand odours" of his old village. This contrasts with the <u>dullness</u> of Scrooge's present life.

Chapter Analysis — The First of the Three Spirits

Fezziwig is an example of a good boss

© Michael Le Poer Trench/ArenaPAL

1) The spirit shows Scrooge a vision of a Christmas Eve <u>party</u>, thrown when Scrooge was an <u>apprentice</u> to Mr Fezziwig. Scrooge enjoys re-living the party again.

2) Scrooge speaks "like his former, not his latter, self" when he defends Fezziwig's <u>generosity</u> to the spirit. This suggests that Scrooge didn't used to think that money was more important than <u>happiness</u> — and his attitude could be changing back.

3) Scrooge begins to understand the <u>effects</u> of his meanness towards Bob Cratchit, and the <u>power</u> that he has to <u>improve</u> Bob's life. Fezziwig gives Scrooge an example of the kind of <u>boss</u> that he could choose to be.

The reader sees that Scrooge has a sad past

'Avarice' is another word for greed — usually in relation to money or material goods.

1) The following vision shows Scrooge "in the prime of life", but he doesn't <u>look</u> it — his face shows "signs of care and <u>avarice</u>". Becoming obsessed with money has physically <u>aged</u> him.

2) His <u>fiancée</u>, Belle, is breaking off their <u>engagement</u> because Scrooge has "<u>changed</u>". She sees that his love of money is becoming more powerful than his "nobler aspirations".

3) Belle knows Scrooge well — she guesses that his <u>coldness</u> comes from his "<u>fear</u>" of the world. Belle clearly loved Scrooge deeply — this helps the reader see that Scrooge wasn't always unlovable and <u>hints</u> that he can change.

Character — Scrooge

Scrooge <u>fears</u> poverty — he says that there's nothing "so hard as poverty". It's this fear that drives him to <u>greed</u> and <u>selfishness</u>.

Belle's family represent the life Scrooge could have had

1) Scrooge sees Belle's <u>daughter</u>, and <u>regrets</u> never having had <u>children</u>. It makes him sad, and his sight grows "very dim".

Theme — Family

Scrooge <u>mourns</u> the loss of the family he never had. Dickens shows that a family can bring <u>comfort</u> and <u>joy</u>.

2) Belle's husband describes seeing Scrooge in his <u>office</u>, "Quite alone in the world". This depiction of a lonely Scrooge <u>contrasts</u> with the happiness of Belle's family.

3) Scrooge is <u>upset</u> by these scenes — he begs the spirit in a "broken voice" to <u>end</u> the visions. It's now clear that Scrooge <u>does</u> care about family and love — but the choices he's made have left him <u>lonely</u> instead.

4) Scrooge tries to get the spirit to put its <u>cap</u> on again — but this time he tries to <u>force</u> it onto its head. He's trying to shut out the truth of his past again — it's <u>painful</u> for him to remember it.

Write about how Scrooge reacts to each vision...

Scrooge sees scenes from his past, and it helps him to learn how to empathise with the people in his present-day life. This is key to his character's development, so make sure you look at his reactions closely.

Chapter Analysis — The Second of the Three Spirits

It's time for Chapter Three, and Scrooge's journey of self-discovery is well underway. In this chapter, the Ghost of Christmas Present pops in for a chat — and shows Scrooge a few more festive visions.

Scrooge's room is transformed

1) The clock strikes one again, to indicate that a <u>new section</u> of the story is about to begin.

Writer's Techniques

Dickens <u>describes</u> the Christmas decorations in great <u>detail</u>. This level of detail helps the reader to visualise the scene.

2) Scrooge <u>finds</u> the Ghost of Christmas Present in the room next to his bedroom. The room is <u>filled</u> with lots of <u>Christmas</u> decor, including holly, mistletoe, ivy, a blazing fire and all kinds of food.

3) There's a huge <u>abundance</u> of food in the room, and in the <u>shops</u> that the spirit and Scrooge visit. Dickens is emphasising that there's <u>plenty</u> of food for everyone, and that no-one should go hungry at Christmas.

The ghost teaches Scrooge the spirit of Christmas

1) In the chapter, the spirit shows Scrooge people <u>celebrating</u> Christmas in lots of different places. Even those who are poor, sick, or separated from their families are cheerful and good-humoured. Dickens emphasises that Christmas is a <u>special</u> time of year, from which even the most <u>disadvantaged</u> people can benefit.

2) The ghost sprinkles drops of "<u>incense</u>" from his torch over homes, hospitals, jails, and almshouses (charitable housing for the poor and elderly), and over anyone who begins to argue. When this happens, their "<u>good humour</u>" is "restored directly".

Theme — The Christmas Spirit

The Ghost of Christmas Present shows that Christmas has a <u>transforming</u> effect on people, encouraging them to do acts of <u>goodwill</u> and <u>charity</u>.

3) The ghost shows Scrooge that Christmas can help to <u>bring people together</u> and improve people's <u>moods</u>.

The Cratchits show the importance of family

1) Scrooge and the ghost visit <u>Bob Cratchit's house</u>, and the Ghost of Christmas Present <u>blesses</u> his house.

Theme — Social Responsibility

The spirit has a particular <u>sympathy</u> for the poor. Its desire to help those that <u>need it most</u> reinforces Dickens's message.

2) The Cratchits' Christmas celebration is full of <u>happiness</u>. As their Christmas Day draws to a <u>close</u>, the Cratchits are "happy, grateful, pleased with one another, and contented with the time". Their lack of money doesn't <u>matter</u> as long as they have each other.

3) Tiny Tim is presented as an <u>innocent</u> victim of the Cratchits' poverty — he's <u>unwell</u>, and the Cratchits are <u>unable</u> to make him better.

Theme — Social Responsibility

In Chapter One, Scrooge believes that the <u>poor</u> and the destitute belong in workhouses or prisons — but the Cratchits show him that they <u>deserve</u> better.

© WATERBURY FILMS/CINEMA CENTER FILMS / THE KOBAL COLLECTION

4) Bob sits <u>close</u> to Tim as if he "dreaded that he might be taken from him". This gives the reader an idea of how badly Bob will take Tim's death, which the spirit warns will happen <u>by the next Christmas</u> if "these shadows <u>remain unaltered</u> by the Future".

Chapter Analysis — The Second of the Three Spirits

Scrooge has to face up to his former opinions

1) Scrooge is <u>upset</u> to find out that Tiny Tim is destined to die. The spirit reminds Scrooge that until now, he didn't <u>care</u> about the plight of poor people — he described them as "surplus population".

2) The spirit says that Scrooge's life may be "<u>more worthless</u>" than that of Tiny Tim and others like him. This forces him to be <u>humble</u> and not have such a <u>high opinion</u> of himself compared to others (especially the poor).

3) Scrooge's concern for Tim <u>teaches</u> him that the poor are real people — not just a <u>problem</u> to be dealt with. He begins to understand the value of <u>charity</u> towards the poor.

Dickens believed that poor people deserved better than to be written off as "surplus population" — see p.7 for more.

Scrooge sees himself through other people's eyes

1) As well as the Cratchits' dinner, the ghost also takes Scrooge to see Fred's Christmas party. Both parties are full of <u>merriment</u>, but at both gatherings Scrooge is the source of <u>resentment</u> or <u>ridicule</u>.

2) Although Bob Cratchit generously insists that his family drink to the <u>health</u> of his boss, Scrooge is thought of as the "<u>Ogre</u>" of the family, who causes a "<u>dark shadow</u>" to pass over the party.

3) Fred and his family and friends laugh "heartily" about Scrooge's actions — they don't take him <u>seriously</u>. However, Fred says he feels <u>sorry</u> for Scrooge — he sees that Scrooge's behaviour is only hurting himself.

4) Fred's family <u>toast</u> Scrooge too, which makes Scrooge feel "light of heart". Fred calls him "Uncle Scrooge" — this is a reminder for Scrooge that he can still be part of a <u>family</u>.

Ignorance and Want link to poverty

1) Just before the spirit leaves, Scrooge sees two "meagre, ragged" children <u>hidden</u> in the spirit's robes. The spirit calls the children <u>Ignorance</u> and <u>Want</u>. They're <u>disturbing</u> to look at — "menacing" and "horrible".

2) Ignorance and Want are <u>symbols</u> of the problems caused by poverty in Victorian society. The spirit says it's the fault of <u>mankind</u> that Ignorance and Want <u>exist</u>.

3) The ghost warns Scrooge to <u>beware</u> of Ignorance and Want — he claims that ignoring the problem will eventually lead to society's "<u>Doom</u>".

> **Theme — Social Responsibility**
>
> The spirit <u>warns</u> Scrooge about the <u>dangers</u> of ignorance in particular. Dickens believed that <u>ignorance</u> was one of the big causes of poverty, and that <u>education</u> was important in helping people to <u>escape</u> it.

4) Scrooge desperately asks whether there's anything that will <u>help</u> Ignorance and Want. The spirit, by <u>reminding</u> Scrooge of his own words ("Are there no prisons?... Are there no workhouses?"), implies that the attitude of heartless people like Scrooge means that there <u>isn't any help</u> available.

"Are there no prisons?... Are there no workhouses?"

This chapter is a pretty cheerful one, especially with Fred's laughter-filled party, but that changes when Ignorance and Want appear. This change in tone forces the reader to pay attention to what they represent.

Chapter Analysis — The Last of the Spirits

Dickens was inventive with his chapter titles, wasn't he? First, second, last... At least it's easy to remember. This chapter has the Ghost of Christmas Yet to Come showing Scrooge — you guessed it — more visions...

The third spirit is much more sinister

1) The last ghost appears. It's completely <u>silent</u>, and its appearance <u>terrifies</u> Scrooge, who's filled with a "horror" and "solemn dread".

2) Scrooge is <u>afraid</u> of the spirit, but he knows that he's going to <u>learn</u> something from it, so he's <u>humble</u> — he bends down on his knees in front of it, and says he'll go with it "with a thankful heart".

3) Scrooge hopes to see <u>himself</u> in the future, having <u>changed</u> his life and become "another man". Scrooge seems to have <u>rejected</u> his old ways, and he believes that the future he'll see will show a more <u>positive</u> picture.

© Nigel Norrington / ArenaPAL

Scrooge sees the consequences of a lonely life

1) Scrooge sees the reactions of some merchants to the death of an <u>unknown man</u>. They're not <u>upset</u> by the death and are utterly uncaring. One of the men says he'll go to the funeral — but only for a <u>free lunch</u>.

2) The ghost then shows Scrooge a group of people who are trying to <u>sell</u> the man's belongings. They claim that if he wanted to keep them after his <u>death</u>, he should've been less "wicked" in <u>life</u> — then he wouldn't have died <u>alone</u>, and someone would've been there to <u>look after</u> his belongings.

Writer's Techniques

The thieves are <u>uncaring</u> — they're more interested in "<u>profit</u>" than the dead man. They <u>mirror</u> Scrooge's own obsession with wealth.

3) The spirit shows Scrooge the man's <u>body</u> in a lonely room "plundered and bereft; unwatched, unwept, uncared for", and he sees the final <u>consequences</u> of leading a <u>selfish</u> life. However, Scrooge doesn't lift the cover over the man's face to see who he is.

4) Scrooge wants to see someone who <u>cares</u> about the man's death, so the ghost shows him a young couple who owe the man money, and who feel "<u>delight</u>" about his death. They're <u>good</u> people, and they don't like <u>rejoicing</u> over a death — but he was such a "merciless" creditor that his death has given them <u>hope</u>.

The story of the young couple's debt has similarities with Dickens's own life — see p.6 for more.

5) Dickens builds <u>suspense</u> by hinting that Scrooge is the dead man — Scrooge is <u>missing</u> from his usual spots, such as his office, and the dead man seems to be as <u>hated</u> as Scrooge. However, Scrooge doesn't realise the dead man is him — he thinks the ghost is showing someone <u>similar</u> to him, to teach him a <u>lesson</u>.

Writer's Techniques

This is an example of <u>dramatic irony</u>, which makes the chapter more thrilling. The reader <u>knows</u> something that Scrooge <u>doesn't</u>, so they have to <u>wait</u> for Scrooge to come to the same conclusion.

Dramatic irony is when the reader knows something that the character doesn't know.

Chapter Analysis — The Last of the Spirits

Tiny Tim's death is a contrast to Scrooge's

1) The spirit takes Scrooge to the Cratchit house after Scrooge asks to see "some tenderness connect with a death" — he's sick of seeing nobody mourning the dead man.

© Clive Barda / ArenaPAL

2) Tiny Tim has died, and the Cratchit house is "quiet". The family talk sadly until Bob breaks down crying and has to leave the room. This contrasts with the uncaring reactions we see in response to Scrooge's own death.

3) Tim will be buried somewhere "green", but the graveyard where Scrooge is buried is "worthy" of the "wretched man" who's buried there — it's "overrun" by "weeds", and "choked up" with lots of graves.

4) Tim and Scrooge's burial places reflect the affection of the people they leave behind.

Seeing the future convinces Scrooge to change

1) The future that the spirit shows to Scrooge is a frightening one — Scrooge doesn't want to die alone and unloved.

Theme — Redemption

Scrooge is so scared by the visions of the future because he thinks they mean he's "past all hope". Dickens suggests that it's never too late to change.

2) The ghost isn't completely unfriendly — its "kind hand" trembles when Scrooge gets more upset. This reminds us that its purpose in showing Scrooge his fate is to help him.

3) Scrooge doesn't know for sure if he can change the future, and the gravestone in the graveyard already has his name on it, which would seem to suggest his future is already set. He's willing to try anyway though — he's desperate to try to avoid his current fate, but he also genuinely wants to become a better man.

The dramatic tension comes to a peak

KEY EVENT

1) Scrooge is determined to change his future but the phantom vanishes without reassuring him.

2) Scrooge gets more and more agitated towards the end of the chapter — he tries desperately to force the ghost to tell him what will happen, but the ghost says nothing.

3) As the drama builds, and Scrooge is holding his hands up "in a last prayer", the action suddenly stops, and the spirit changes into a bedpost. This puts a sudden end to the dramatic tension in the chapter, and leaves the reader wondering what's going to happen next.

Writer's Techniques

The chapter ends on a cliff-hanger — we don't know for certain if Scrooge will be able to change his future and save himself. This adds tension to the story.

KEY QUOTE

"Oh, tell me I may sponge away the writing on this stone!"

Yes, yes, we get it — it's rubbish being poor, good people die, and Scrooge has no friends. This whole section is a bit depressing, actually — luckily things get a whole lot more cheerful in the next chapter.

Section Two — Discussion of Chapters

Chapter Analysis — The End of It

And here it is — the end of the book. In this chapter, Scrooge follows through on all the changes he's promised to make. It's a classic happy ending — nobody dies, families are reunited, *and* it's Christmas.

Scrooge is a new man

1) Scrooge finds himself back in his own bed. He repeats his <u>promise</u> to "live in the Past, the Present, and the Future!" — he's still <u>committed</u> to changing.

2) This chapter is a <u>new beginning</u> for Scrooge. He says he's "quite a baby" — as if he has been <u>reborn</u> into a new life.

3) Scrooge finds out that it's still <u>Christmas Day</u> — so he has a <u>chance</u> to spend Christmas the way it should be spent.

4) Dickens uses <u>similes</u> to present Scrooge's <u>happiness</u> and <u>relief</u> in a vivid way: he's "as light as a feather," "as happy as an angel", "as merry as a school-boy", and "as giddy as a drunken man".

5) The weather <u>changes</u> again to match Scrooge's <u>temperament</u> — there's "golden sunlight", and it's "clear", "bright", and "jovial" outside. This also adds to the joyful mood of the chapter — the reader can sense that the <u>ending</u> will be happy because of the <u>changed setting</u>.

Theme — Redemption

In Chapter Five, Scrooge puts everything he's learnt into practice — his redemption is <u>complete</u>, and now he's a <u>better man</u>.

© KINGWILL Marilyn/ArenaPAL

There are parallels with Chapter One

1) Scrooge's <u>attitude</u> has completely <u>changed</u> from the beginning of the novel — he's cheerful, friendly and generous towards everyone he meets.

2) To show this, Dickens takes elements from the first chapter, and <u>reintroduces</u> them, but with a <u>twist</u>. The novel has a <u>circular structure</u> — this helps the reader <u>compare</u> how Scrooge has become a better man:

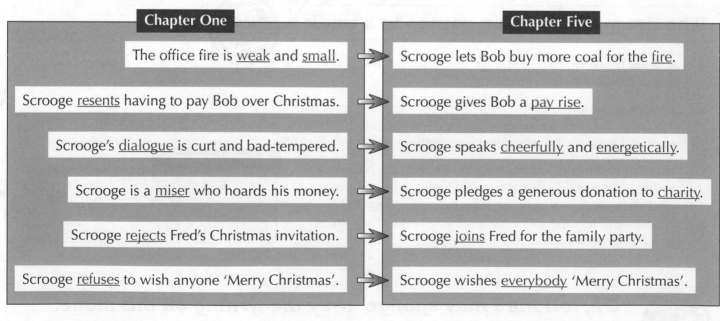

Chapter One	Chapter Five
The office fire is <u>weak</u> and <u>small</u>.	Scrooge lets Bob buy more coal for the <u>fire</u>.
Scrooge <u>resents</u> having to pay Bob over Christmas.	Scrooge gives Bob a <u>pay rise</u>.
Scrooge's <u>dialogue</u> is curt and bad-tempered.	Scrooge speaks <u>cheerfully</u> and <u>energetically</u>.
Scrooge is a <u>miser</u> who hoards his money.	Scrooge pledges a generous donation to <u>charity</u>.
Scrooge <u>rejects</u> Fred's Christmas invitation.	Scrooge <u>joins</u> Fred for the family party.
Scrooge <u>refuses</u> to wish anyone 'Merry Christmas'.	Scrooge wishes <u>everybody</u> 'Merry Christmas'.

3) The final chapter allows Scrooge to <u>prove</u> how he's transformed, by <u>righting the wrongs</u> of his former self.

Chapter Analysis — The End of It

Money isn't the most important thing to Scrooge any more

1) Scrooge meets one of the charity collectors in the street, and donates a large amount of money to their cause. He says that it's "very kind" of them to do the work they do.

2) Scrooge offers to help the Cratchit family in this chapter — he sees that it's his responsibility to help people who are worse off than him.

3) Dickens uses the transformation of Scrooge to help his readers to understand the importance of helping the poor. Scrooge is now more interested in helping other people, and he realises that he can do this by being generous with his money.

> **Theme — Social Responsibility**
>
> At the beginning of the story, Scrooge represents the uncaring rich people of Victorian society. By the end, he represents how Dickens feels the well-off should act towards the poor.

Scrooge learns to honour Christmas...

1) Scrooge says that Christmas should be "praised" for his transformation — his understanding of the Christmas spirit is one of the things that has made him change.

2) Scrooge walks down the street with a "delighted smile". This makes the people he passes greet him with a cheery "merry Christmas to you!" Scrooge is already spreading the Christmas spirit to others, as the Ghost of Christmas Present taught him.

3) Scrooge buys a huge turkey for Bob Cratchit, so that he and his family can celebrate Christmas more lavishly.

> **Theme — The Christmas Spirit**
>
> In this chapter, Scrooge applies everything he's learnt from the ghosts about the Christmas spirit — he celebrates the day with love, generosity and kindness.

> Scrooge is selfless — he doesn't ask for thanks from the charity collector, and he sends the turkey to Bob anonymously. He's being charitable because it's the right thing to do, not because he wants any credit for it.

© KINGWILL Marilyn/ArenaPAL

...and he gets a family again

1) Scrooge goes to Fred's house for Christmas. Despite his previous behaviour, Scrooge is welcomed. Fred shakes his hand enthusiastically, and they celebrate Christmas with "wonderful unanimity".

2) Dickens uses the acceptance of Fred and his family to illustrate that family love is unconditional, and can be the source of "won-der-ful happiness!"

3) Scrooge also gains another family — he becomes a "second father" to Tiny Tim. In Chapter Two, Scrooge was upset that he never became a father — helping Tiny Tim and the Cratchits has allowed him to achieve that dream.

'Unanimity' means unity or agreement.

> **Theme — Family**
>
> Scrooge has become a part of two families. He's realised that having a family is important to him.

EXAM TIP

Look at the structure of the novel...

Impress the examiner by talking about structure. The stuff about the novel's circular structure on p.20 is really important, but think about other things too — like how each ghost gets its own chapter. See p.46 for more.

Practice Questions

And... exhale. We're officially done breaking down the chapters of 'A Christmas Carol', so you're in for another treat — it's question time. Just write a sentence or two for your answers to these questions — there are some more detailed questions over the page for you to get your teeth into later. If you find you can't remember something, have a flick back through the section to find out what you need to know.

Quick Questions

1) Who was Jacob Marley? How does Scrooge know him?

2) Give three examples of Scrooge's actions in the first chapter which show his unpleasant personality.

3) List three supernatural events that occur before the arrival of Marley's ghost.

4) Find a quote from the novel that suggests Fezziwig is a generous man.

5) Why does Belle release Scrooge from his engagement to her?

6) What does the Ghost of Christmas Present do that improves people's moods?

7) The Ghost of Christmas Present echoes some of the things that Scrooge said in Chapter One in order to teach him a lesson. Give an example of something the spirit says to Scrooge.

8) How does Scrooge react to the appearance of the Ghost of Christmas Yet to Come?

9) Is the Ghost of Christmas Yet to Come completely unsympathetic to Scrooge?

10) Give an example from either Chapter Three or Chapter Four of a character who:
   a) makes fun of Scrooge
   b) is kind about Scrooge

11) List three things that Scrooge does to improve Bob Cratchit's life in Chapter Five.

12) Briefly explain what the narrator tells us about Scrooge's future.

Practice Questions

More questions! This time you'll need to write a bit more, so don't do them all at once — aim for about a paragraph for the in-depth questions, and a longer essay for the exam-style ones.

In-depth Questions

1) Explain the ways in which Marley and Scrooge are similar characters, and why it's significant that they have so much in common.

2) How does Dickens use the weather in Chapter One of the novel?

3) Explain why it is significant that Fred is Fan's son.

4) What do Ignorance and Want represent? Give reasons to support your answer.

5) Explain how Dickens uses dramatic irony in Chapter Four.

6) Pick three of Scrooge's actions in Chapter Five, and explain what they show about his changed personality.

Exam-Style Questions

1) Read the passage in Chapter Two that begins "And now Scrooge looked on more attentively than ever," and ends "'Spirit!' said Scrooge in a broken voice, 'remove me from this place.'"

   Using this extract, discuss how Dickens presents Scrooge as a lonely figure in *A Christmas Carol*. Write about:
   a) the way Scrooge is presented in this extract, and
   b) the way Scrooge is presented in the novel as a whole.

2) "In *A Christmas Carol,* rich people are always evil and poor people are always good."
   To what extent do you agree with the above statement?

3) To what extent is Scrooge the only victim of his selfishness?

4) Read the passage in Chapter Four that starts "The Phantom slowly, gravely, silently approached." and ends with "'Lead on, Spirit!'"

   Discuss the way that Scrooge interacts with all of the ghosts in the novel. You should talk about the above extract in your answer, as well as the rest of the book.

Section Three — Characters

Character Profile — Ebenezer Scrooge

Scrooge is the main character in *A Christmas Carol,* so you're going to need to know him inside out.
He starts the novel as a rude miser — but he ends up a changed character, and an all-round nice bloke.

Scrooge doesn't seem to care about anything except money

1) At the start of the novel Scrooge is portrayed very <u>negatively</u>, as someone who only cares about <u>money</u> — he's described as "a squeezing, wrenching, grasping, scraping, clutching, covetous old sinner!"

2) He's so <u>miserly</u> and <u>mean</u> that he begrudges Bob Cratchit his Christmas wages, and won't allow him a decent fire.

3) In a vision of Scrooge's <u>past</u>, his fiancée, Belle, says that Scrooge sees money as an "<u>Idol</u>", and that it has "displaced" her in Scrooge's affections. This suggests that Scrooge worships money as if it's a <u>god</u>, and his love for it is greater than his love for Belle.

> **At the start, Scrooge is...**
>
> **bitter:** "No wind that blew was bitterer than he".
>
> **cynical:** "What's Christmas time to you but a time for paying bills without money".
>
> **isolated:** "secret and self-contained, and solitary as an oyster".

He's cold-hearted and unfeeling

1) Scrooge is <u>unsympathetic</u> towards other people, so he has no interest in helping the poor. He refuses to donate to <u>charity</u> — he thinks he's done enough by paying <u>taxes</u> to support the prisons and workhouses.

2) He's <u>indifferent</u> to how poor people might feel, and he believes it's not his "<u>business</u>" to <u>care</u> about them.

3) Dickens describes Scrooge using <u>cold</u> and <u>icy</u> language — there's a "<u>cold</u> within him" that "froze his old features", and he's described as having a "frosty rime" (a frosty covering). This association with the cold emphasises Scrooge's <u>cold-hearted</u> nature.

© Ray Tang/REX

We learn that Scrooge's past has shaped him

1) As the reader sees more of Scrooge's past, it becomes easier to <u>understand</u> why Scrooge is so cold and bitter — the events of his past are partly <u>responsible</u> for his present-day personality.

2) Scrooge is shown <u>sympathetically</u> as "a lonely boy" near a "feeble fire" at his old school. We learn that he's been <u>left</u> there because his father won't let him come home for Christmas.

3) Scrooge is eventually brought home by his sister, who he clearly had a <u>close relationship</u> with. It's possible that he <u>isolates</u> himself from Fred because he's a sad <u>reminder</u> of the sister Scrooge has lost.

4) Scrooge is <u>distressed</u> at the vision of Belle leaving him, and this painful memory is made worse by the vision of Belle's <u>happy family</u>. The reader feels <u>sympathy</u> when he pleads "in a broken voice" to be shown no more. It seems like the <u>heartbreak</u> Scrooge suffered may have contributed to his bitter, closed-off personality in Chapter One.

> **Theme — Redemption**
>
> Scrooge's <u>past</u> suggests that people aren't necessarily born <u>bad</u> — and that <u>even</u> someone like Scrooge can have <u>goodness</u> inside of them.

Character Profile — Ebenezer Scrooge

Scrooge has to see himself as others see him

1) Throughout the visions, Scrooge is forced to see how <u>other people</u> talk about him when he's not around:

- Mrs Cratchit calls Scrooge an "odious, stingy, hard, unfeeling man".
- Fred says he's "a <u>comical</u> old fellow", and "not so <u>pleasant</u> as he might be".
- A businessman calls Scrooge "Old Scratch" — a nickname for the <u>devil</u>.
- A couple, who owe Scrooge money, call him "<u>merciless</u>".

2) At the <u>beginning</u> of the novel, Scrooge is <u>selfish</u> — he doesn't care about how his attitude to life affects others. However, the spirits show him the way other people <u>talk</u> about him, which makes him realise his <u>faults</u> and convinces him to change his <u>attitude</u>.

Tiny Tim shows Scrooge that the poor are people too

1) Seeing Tiny Tim helps Scrooge to feel <u>empathy</u> again. Scrooge asks the spirit if Tim will die, with "an interest he had <u>never felt before</u>" — Tim's situation makes Scrooge start to care about other people.

2) The Ghost of Christmas Present uses Tim to show Scrooge how <u>wrong</u> his beliefs about "surplus population" are, and to force him to think about poor people as <u>individuals</u>. Scrooge is saddened by how <u>cruel</u> his opinions were.

3) Scrooge is "overcome with penitence and grief" when he realises how <u>wrong</u> he's been. He starts to accept that helping people like Tim is his <u>responsibility</u>.

© Ray Tang/REX

Scrooge's values change

1) Scrooge's character <u>changes</u> completely by the end of the novel. He <u>laughs</u> at himself and says he's "as merry as a school-boy".

2) He also learns to be <u>charitable</u>. He buys the Cratchits a Christmas turkey and makes a large donation to charity.

3) Scrooge completely changes his mind about <u>Christmas</u> — the <u>narrator</u> says that he "knew how to keep Christmas well".

4) The spirits teach Scrooge to <u>value family</u> and <u>companionship</u>, so he embraces his nephew's family and becomes a father figure to Tiny Tim.

Scrooge becomes...

generous: "I'll raise your salary".

happy: "Scrooge regarded every one with a delighted smile".

sociable: "Wonderful party, wonderful games, wonderful unanimity".

 EXAM TIP

Show that you understand how Scrooge changes...

The whole of *A Christmas Carol* revolves around Scrooge — the structure of the novel is based around the way he gradually changes into a better man. It's important to show the examiner that you understand this.

Character Profile — Jacob Marley

Jacob Marley used to be Scrooge's business partner — and now he's a ghost. Much like Scrooge, he wasn't particularly nice when he was alive, so now he's doomed to roam the world forever. Bet his feet hurt.

Marley's ghost has come to warn Scrooge

© KINGWILL Marilyn/ArenaPAL

1) Marley's main role in the novel is to <u>warn</u> Scrooge about what will happen after he dies — unless he <u>changes</u>.

2) Marley and Scrooge have <u>similar</u> personalities — they're "two kindred spirits", who are obsessed with money and don't care about other people. They're so similar that Scrooge lives in Marley's <u>old rooms</u> and even answers to Marley's <u>name</u> — "it was all the same to him". These similarities emphasise Marley's role as a <u>warning</u> figure.

3) Marley's <u>punishment</u> is the consequence of a self-centred, "misused" life. Dickens has already shown <u>Scrooge</u> behaving similarly — so Marley's fate illustrates what will happen to Scrooge if he doesn't <u>change</u>.

Marley's appearance is disturbing

1) Scrooge feels "the chilling influence" of Marley's "death-cold eyes", and when the ghost removes the bandage from its head, its "lower jaw dropped down upon its breast" — a <u>horrible</u> image. Marley's <u>terrifying</u> appearance reflects the frightening nature of his <u>message</u>, and makes it seem more <u>important</u>.

Marley is...

terrifying: "the spectre's voice disturbed the very marrow in his bones".

exhausted: "I cannot rest, I cannot stay, I cannot linger anywhere".

direct: "I am here tonight to warn you".

2) Marley gives off an "<u>infernal</u>" (hellish) atmosphere, and his clothes are "agitated as by the <u>hot vapour</u> from an oven". This description links Marley to ideas of <u>Hell</u> and eternal suffering.

3) The chain Marley wears is made of <u>money-related objects</u>. It was forged because he <u>cared</u> more about money than people. The chain is particularly disturbing for Scrooge because Marley tells him that he bears a similar, but <u>larger</u>, chain.

Marley tries to help Scrooge

1) Marley <u>regrets</u> that he didn't change his ways whilst he was alive — it's <u>too late</u> for him to avoid suffering. All he can do is offer Scrooge the chance to escape the same fate.

Theme — Redemption

Scrooge is <u>lucky</u> — Marley implies that most people are already doomed to their fates, but Scrooge will get one last chance at <u>redemption</u>.

2) He has stood invisibly at Scrooge's shoulder for "many a day" in the past. He acts as a kind of <u>hellish guardian angel</u> to Scrooge.

3) Marley says that his presence now is "a chance and <u>hope</u>" of his own "procuring". This suggests that he's <u>tried</u> (and succeeded) to find a way to help Scrooge and give him a <u>chance</u> to save himself.

4) Marley is acting <u>selflessly</u> — he's helping a friend, even though he has no hope of <u>redemption</u> himself.

KEY QUOTE

"I wear the chain I forged in life... I made it link by link"

Marley's scary to look at, but give him a break — he's not exactly got time to do his make-up, seeing as he's a bit busy with his eternal damnation. He also regrets his past life, and he's trying to help Scrooge.

Character Profile — Fred

Fred is Scrooge's nephew, and his only living family — he's the son of Scrooge's sister, Fan. Fred never seems to be particularly put off by his uncle's grumpiness — he feels sorry for him instead.

Fred is a complete contrast to Scrooge

1) Fred arrives in Scrooge's offices "all in a glow" and "his eyes sparkled" — this emphasises the <u>warmth</u> and friendliness of his character. He's the <u>opposite</u> of Scrooge, who's associated with the cold.

2) Fred <u>disagrees</u> with Scrooge's miserly values. He thinks that Scrooge's wealth is useless because "he don't do any <u>good</u> with it" — suggesting that, unlike Scrooge, he values <u>happiness</u> more than money.

3) He's <u>empathetic</u> — he's "heartily <u>sorry</u>" for the Cratchit family after Tim dies, even though he barely knows them. This contrasts with Scrooge, who begins the novel as a <u>self-centred</u> person who doesn't care about others.

4) Dickens uses Fred as a <u>foil</u> to Scrooge's character. The differences between them <u>emphasise</u> Scrooge's negative qualities.

A foil is a character who may share similarities, but also some important differences, with another character. This emphasises each character's key characteristics.

© Nigel Norrington / ArenaPAL

Fred is a cheerful man

1) Fred's personality is <u>defined</u> by his distinctive and pleasant <u>laugh</u>. The narrator says he'd like to meet "a man more blest in a laugh than Scrooge's nephew". Fred's laugh illustrates his <u>cheerfulness</u> and <u>optimism</u>.

2) He's <u>even-tempered</u> and <u>refuses</u> to argue with Scrooge. He tells Scrooge "I'll keep my Christmas humour to the last", and later says that he "couldn't be angry" with Scrooge if he tried.

3) Fred shows <u>insight</u> when he says that Scrooge's "offences carry their own punishment" — he understands that by refusing to embrace his <u>family</u>, Scrooge is only hurting <u>himself</u>.

4) He's <u>determined</u> to include Scrooge in the celebrations: "I mean to give him the same chance, every year, whether he likes it or not". He believes in the <u>importance</u> of being <u>kind</u> at Christmas, especially to family.

Fred shows true Christmas spirit

1) Dickens <u>presents</u> Fred as someone who shows lots of the values associated with <u>Christmas</u> and the Christmas spirit.

2) Fred shows <u>generosity</u> to Scrooge in inviting him to his party, and <u>forgiveness</u> when he welcomes Scrooge into his home, <u>despite</u> Scrooge's behaviour — "It is a mercy he didn't shake his arm off".

3) Fred also knows how to have <u>fun</u> — his Christmas party is an enjoyable occasion, which is filled with games and laughter.

Fred is...

jovial: "Scrooge's nephew revelled in another laugh".

enthusiastic: "A merry Christmas uncle! God save you!"

caring: "Bob told them of the extraordinary kindness of Mr Scrooge's nephew".

EXAM TIP

Talk about the contrast between Fred and Scrooge...

Mentioning how different Fred and Scrooge are shows that you understand the purpose of Fred's character in the novel, and correctly using terms like 'foil' will show the examiner that you really know your stuff.

Character Profile — The Ghosts

The Ghosts of Christmas Past, Present, and Yet to Come can be tricky to get your head around, but they're important — they symbolise some complex stuff, and they're a big part of the wider message in the novel.

The three ghosts are different — but they all help Scrooge

1) Dickens characterises the three ghosts very differently, which adds <u>interest</u> and <u>variety</u> to the story. The first ghost is a <u>contradictory</u> figure, who's both strong and gentle at the same time. The second ghost is a cheerful, <u>jolly</u> giant — and in contrast, the third ghost is silent and <u>ominous</u>.

2) The ghosts exist <u>outside</u> the boundaries of human <u>time</u>, and they show Scrooge visions of the past, present, and future. This gives the novel a <u>magical</u>, <u>dream-like</u> mood.

3) Scrooge <u>learns</u> from each of his encounters with the ghosts. They make him realise what the impact and consequences of his past and present behaviour could be.

> **Writer's Techniques**
>
> Dickens uses the appearances of the <u>ghosts</u> to reinforce the <u>structure</u> of the novel. Each ghost has its own <u>chapter</u>, which focuses on either Scrooge's past, present or future.

The Ghost of Christmas Past represents memory and truth

1) The Ghost of Christmas Past's appearance is a strange mixture of child-like and aged. It's <u>connected</u>, through Scrooge's <u>memory</u>, to different stages of Scrooge's life.

2) A "bright, clear jet of <u>light</u>" shines from its head — this light could symbolise the <u>truth</u> that can be found in <u>memories</u>.

3) The ghost is strong but <u>quiet</u>. Its voice is "<u>low</u>" as if "it were at a distance" — like it's speaking to Scrooge from somewhere <u>far away</u>, or <u>long ago</u>. This emphasises the spirit's connection to Scrooge's distant past.

4) The ghost helps the reader <u>sympathise</u> with Scrooge by showing us that parts of his childhood were <u>miserable</u>, and that he wasn't always so cold and unfeeling.

© Clive Barda / ArenaPAL

The first spirit is forceful to help Scrooge change

1) The spirit <u>makes</u> Scrooge <u>explain</u> the things that he realises when he sees the visions of his past. For example, its insistent <u>questions</u> ("What is the matter?... Something, I think?") force Scrooge to explain what he's realised after Fezziwig's party — that sometimes it's <u>important</u> to spend <u>money</u> generously, because of the happiness it gives to others.

2) The memory of Belle is "torture" for Scrooge — he <u>begs</u> the ghost to let him <u>leave</u>, but the spirit is too strong for him — it "pinioned him in both his arms" and "<u>forced</u>" him to watch. The ghost's actions seem cruel, but its actions help Scrooge to <u>learn</u>.

> **The Ghost of Christmas Past is...**
>
> **forceful:** "But the relentless Ghost pinioned him in both his arms, and forced him to observe".
>
> **questioning:** "Is that so much that he deserves this praise?"
>
> **mysterious:** "It was a strange figure".

Character Profile — The Ghosts

The Ghost of Christmas Present generously helps others

1) The Ghost of Christmas Present is <u>compassionate</u>. It sprinkles incense and water from its torch as a <u>blessing</u>, and it restores the "<u>good humour</u>" of angry people so that they can enjoy Christmas.

2) The ghost is closely associated with <u>abundance</u> and <u>generosity</u>. For example, the <u>torch</u> the spirit carries resembles "Plenty's horn" (a symbol of abundance from Greek and Roman mythology) and it <u>generously</u> sprinkles blessings from it on those who need it most.

3) Its <u>scabbard</u> has no sword in it, and it's rusted — suggesting that Christmas should be a time for <u>peace</u>, not fighting other people.

The Ghost of Christmas Present is..

jolly: "there sat a jolly Giant, glorious to see".

friendly: "Come in! and know me better, man!"

severe: "Slander those who tell it ye!"

The second ghost is upset about poverty

© Nigel Norrington / ArenaPAL

1) The Ghost of Christmas Present has "<u>sympathy</u> with all poor men", and is "<u>sorrowful</u>" at the sight of Ignorance and Want. The spirit cares about the poor and it <u>challenges</u> Scrooge's previous harsh words about poverty — calling them "wicked".

2) The spirit speaks emotionally about the way that society <u>ignores</u> the problem of poverty. It argues that society <u>denies</u> the problems of ignorance and want, and suggests that ignoring these problems will eventually lead to society's "Doom".

The Ghost of Christmas Yet to Come is a sinister figure

1) The Ghost of Christmas Yet to Come represents Scrooge's <u>future</u>. The ghost is "shrouded in a deep black garment" — its mysterious appearance implies that the future cannot be <u>known</u> for sure.

The third ghost is similar in appearance to the <u>Grim Reaper</u>, which Victorian readers would've recognised as a symbol of approaching <u>death</u>.

2) The ghost is <u>silent</u> and <u>intimidating</u>. It points instead of speaking, and won't answer Scrooge's questions. This adds to the sense of <u>mystery</u> surrounding it.

The Ghost of Christmas Yet to Come is..

frightening: "Scrooge feared the silent shape so much that his legs trembled beneath him".

mysterious: "it seemed to scatter gloom and mystery".

resolute: "the Spirit did not stay for anything".

3) It's only when Scrooge begins to <u>beg</u> that the ghost shows any kind of reaction at all — its "kind hand trembled". This could suggest that the ghost <u>pities</u> Scrooge, reminding the reader that the ghosts are trying to <u>help</u> him.

EXAM TIP

Think about what the ghosts might symbolise...

The ghosts are mystical creatures, who have an intimate knowledge of Scrooge's life and history. Because of this, Dickens uses them to pack in symbols and deeper messages like sardines, so look at them closely.

Character Profile — The Cratchit Family

Bob Cratchit is Scrooge's clerk. He gets paid a pittance by Scrooge and has to work in poor conditions. Dickens uses Bob and his family to illustrate the social problems that poverty caused in the Victorian era.

The Cratchits are poor but loving

1) Mr and Mrs Cratchit have <u>six</u> children — Martha, Peter, Belinda, two "smaller Cratchits" and Tiny Tim. Except for Martha, they all live in the same four-roomed house. They're <u>loving</u> and <u>cheerful</u> despite their poverty.

2) Dickens's depiction of the Cratchits <u>reminds</u> the reader that poor people are not just a <u>social problem</u> — they're individuals and families who share joys, love, sorrows and fears like anyone else.

> **Theme — Family**
>
> Unlike Scrooge, who's <u>rich</u> but lonely, the Cratchit family are <u>poor</u>, but rich in love. The Cratchits' happiness shows that <u>family</u> and companionship is more likely to bring happiness than <u>money</u>.

Bob Cratchit is Scrooge's employee

© REX

1) As Scrooge's clerk, Bob is <u>uncomplaining</u> and <u>tolerant</u>. He works quietly in his "dismal little cell" of an office despite the bitter cold.

2) He's <u>courteous</u> and <u>deferential</u> — he returns Fred's greetings "cordially" and addresses Scrooge as "sir".

3) Bob is <u>patient</u> when Scrooge grumbles about his taking Christmas day off. Bob remains <u>civil</u> despite Scrooge's continually grumpy attitude.

4) His <u>eagerness</u> and <u>pleasure</u> regarding Christmas contrast with Scrooge's attitude. Bob can't help applauding Fred's speech about the joy of Christmas — which <u>contrasts</u> with Scrooge's grumpy response — "Humbug!"

He's also a kind and devoted father

1) Bob is a <u>good-humoured</u>, <u>playful</u> father. He carries Tiny Tim home from the Christmas church service on his shoulders, and on his way home on Christmas Eve he takes twenty turns sliding down an icy street — despite having no <u>coat</u>.

2) When he thinks Martha isn't joining the family for Christmas, he's <u>upset</u>. He hugs her "to his heart's content" when she appears. It's important to him to have all his <u>family together</u> at Christmas.

3) He's <u>caring</u> and <u>tender</u> with Tiny Tim, who sits "very close to his father's side" while Bob holds his hand.

4) Despite his <u>grief</u> at Tim's death, he tries to be <u>cheerful</u> around his family, in order to spare them more pain — "'I am very happy,' said little Bob."

> **Bob Cratchit is...**
>
> **cheerful:** "Bob was very cheerful with them".
>
> **loving:** "Bob... hugged his daughter to his heart's content".
>
> **forgiving:** "Mr Scrooge, the Founder of the Feast!"

> **Theme — Family**
>
> Bob is very <u>close</u> to his children, <u>especially</u> Tim. This makes his <u>grief</u> at losing him even <u>sadder</u> for the reader.

Character Profile — The Cratchit Family

Mrs Cratchit is good-natured and busy

1) Mrs Cratchit <u>works hard</u> to make the Cratchit family <u>happy</u>. The Christmas goose has to be "eked out" to feed the whole family, but the Cratchits greet the food with "universal admiration".

2) Although she thinks Scrooge is an "odious, stingy, hard, unfeeling man", she still <u>drinks</u> to his health, because Bob wants her to and she <u>loves</u> him.

3) When Tim dies she's <u>protective</u> of her family's feelings. She speaks in a "steady, <u>cheerful</u> voice" and <u>hides</u> her "weak eyes" from Bob — she doesn't want to add to his worries.

> **Writer's Techniques**
>
> The Cratchits are presented as a <u>perfect</u>, good family. Dickens <u>idealises</u> the Cratchits so that his middle and upper class readers would be more likely to <u>sympathise</u> with them than if they were realistic and <u>flawed</u>.

Tiny Tim is frail — but he doesn't complain

1) Tiny Tim is <u>fragile</u> and very <u>ill</u>. His father carries him on his shoulders and is especially <u>close</u> to him, whilst Tim's siblings make sure he joins in all the fun.

2) Dickens presents Tiny Tim as a <u>good</u> character by showing us his <u>religious nature</u>. Tim hopes people see him in church, because he wants to remind people about "who made lame beggars walk" (Jesus). He also echoes his father's <u>toast</u> — "God bless us every one!"

3) Dickens also uses Tim to show how poverty can lead to <u>suffering</u> and <u>death</u>. If Scrooge hadn't helped the Cratchits, Tiny Tim would've <u>died</u>.

Religion was an important part of everyday life in Victorian society — see p.9.

© Ray Tang/REX

The Cratchit children are hard-working

1) Peter is Bob's "son and heir". He likes the idea of being <u>rich</u> and <u>upper class</u> — he proudly wears Bob's "shirt collar", and "yearned to show his linen in the <u>fashionable</u> Parks".

Upper-class Victorians would often ride through public parks, where they could show off their finest clothing to society.

2) Bob is keen for Peter to start <u>working</u> as a "man of business", while Martha works <u>hard</u> as a milliner's apprentice (making hats). Dickens emphasises that the Cratchit children aren't <u>lazy</u> or <u>unwilling</u> to work, to <u>challenge</u> the beliefs of those who thought that poverty was often linked to laziness — see p.7.

3) The Cratchits all <u>help</u> out with the Christmas dinner, even the youngest children — they work together as a <u>family</u>.

4) The young Cratchits are <u>excitable</u> — they "crammed spoons into their mouths, lest they should shriek for goose". Their excitement adds to the <u>positivity</u> of the Cratchit household.

> **Writer's Techniques**
>
> Dickens uses a <u>long sentence</u>, made up of several <u>short clauses</u>, to emphasise how <u>busy</u> the Cratchits are as they make the final preparations for dinner. Look at the sentence that starts "Mrs Cratchit made the gravy...".

KEY QUOTE

"Spirit of Tiny Tim, thy childish essence was from God!"

The Cratchits are a family who deserve better than the poverty they suffer, especially the innocent Tiny Tim. Dickens presents them so positively that it's impossible <u>not</u> to think the poor might deserve something more.

Character Profile — Characters From Scrooge's Past

The Ghost of Christmas Past shows Scrooge a series of visions, all of which have people from his past in them. The characters on this page all had an impact on Scrooge's life — which the spirit forces him to remember.

Fan helps to break Scrooge's isolation

1) Fan was Scrooge's sister, who was <u>affectionate</u>, <u>loving</u> and full of laughter. The ghost and Scrooge agree that "she had a large heart".

2) She had a strong <u>bond</u> with Scrooge — she calls him "Dear, dear brother", and he calls her "quite a woman".

3) Fan had <u>asked</u> her father more than once to <u>allow</u> Scrooge to come home. Her <u>excitement</u> shows how important it is for her to spend Christmas with Scrooge.

4) Fan is <u>dead</u> by the time the <u>main events</u> of the book take place — this makes the reader <u>pity</u> Scrooge for having lost the sister he once loved.

Theme — Family

Fan is eventually able to change her father's mind, which is a <u>parallel</u> to the way that her son, Fred, insists on inviting Scrooge for Christmas <u>every year</u> until he changes his mind. Fan and Fred both want Scrooge to be a part of their <u>family life</u>.

Fezziwig is a businessman with a generous heart

1) Mr Fezziwig was Scrooge's genial, cheerful <u>employer</u> when he was a young apprentice. Fezziwig is used as a <u>contrast</u> to Scrooge — but he's a <u>model</u> for the man that Scrooge later becomes.

2) Fezziwig makes his warehouse "snug, and warm, and dry, and bright" for a Christmas <u>party</u> for family and workers. This contrasts with Scrooge's mean, dark office when he's an <u>employer</u> himself.

Writer's Techniques

Dickens writes that Fezziwig's <u>calves</u> shone "like moons" whilst he <u>danced</u>. This light-hearted <u>simile</u> makes the Fezziwigs' dancing seem humorous and playful.

3) Fezziwig and his wife <u>dance</u> vigorously at the party. He's a jovial, energetic figure.

4) Fezziwig has the <u>power</u> to make people's lives <u>good</u> or <u>bad</u>, and he <u>chooses</u> to make them good. He doesn't spend lots of money on the party, but what he does spend is used to bring <u>joy</u> to others, which creates a great deal of <u>happiness</u>. Scrooge realises this, and begins to do the same in his own life.

Belle tells Scrooge some hard truths

1) Belle was Scrooge's beautiful, wise fiancée. She <u>releases</u> Scrooge from their engagement because she sees he has begun to love <u>money</u> more than her.

2) She's <u>poor</u> and knows that Scrooge, who weighs "everything by Gain", has become reluctant to <u>marry</u> her.

3) This separation is a <u>turning point</u> in Scrooge's life. Belle ends up with a family and a home, which, despite being "not very large or handsome", is "full of comfort". In contrast, Scrooge chooses a <u>lonely</u> life devoted to <u>money</u>.

© iStockphoto.com/laartist

KEY QUOTE

"With a full heart, for the love of him you once were"

Personally, I think "it's not you, it's me" is an easier way to break up with someone, but each to their own. The characters from Scrooge's past show the reader how he used to be important to others and loved.

Character Profile — Other Characters

There are a few more characters who play a role in *A Christmas Carol*. Most of them aren't in the book for long, but it's still important that you know who they are, and why Dickens included them in the novel.

The charity collectors have a sense of social responsibility

1) The charity collectors are two "portly", "pleasant" men who visit Scrooge's offices looking for <u>donations</u> to the <u>poor</u>.

2) They have <u>compassion</u> for the poor, and they show the importance of <u>charity</u> at Christmas — a time when "Want is keenly felt" amongst those in poverty.

3) The charity collectors convey Dickens's <u>belief</u> that prisons and workhouses weren't acceptable places to send the <u>poor</u> — and that many people "would rather <u>die</u>" than go to one. They point out how important it is for people to understand their <u>social responsibility</u> towards those who are <u>less fortunate</u>.

© Moviestore/REX

Joe and the thieves are as greedy and ruthless as Scrooge

1) Joe runs a seedy, disreputable shop in a <u>filthy</u> part of the city.

2) The three <u>thieves</u> who are there have stolen Scrooge's possessions to <u>sell</u> to Joe. They feel <u>justified</u> in doing so — it's "no sin" because Scrooge was such a "wicked old screw" whilst he was alive.

3) They're <u>disrespectful</u> about Scrooge — they <u>laugh</u> about the thefts, and one of them has even taken the <u>shirt</u> from Scrooge's corpse — she says it would have been "wasted" on him.

4) By <u>isolating</u> himself from friends and family, Scrooge has ensured that his possessions end up in the <u>wrong hands</u>. Instead of helping <u>deserving</u> people like the Cratchits, Scrooge's wealth is profiting <u>thieves</u>.

> **Theme — Poverty**
>
> Dickens's <u>description</u> of the area around Joe's shop — which "reeked with crime, with filth, and misery" — is brutal and shocking. He doesn't <u>romanticise</u> poverty here.

The wealthy London businessmen don't care about Scrooge

1) The merchants Scrooge sees in Chapter Four are obsessed by <u>wealth</u>. They play with "great gold seals" and jingle the money in their pockets. Like Scrooge, they represent the <u>greedy rich</u> people of Victorian society.

2) They don't care about Scrooge's <u>death</u> — they don't even use his <u>name</u>, and one says he will only attend the funeral for the <u>free lunch</u>.

3) One merchant has a "<u>monstrous</u> chin" and another has a growth on his nose that "shook like the gills of a turkey-cock". These details <u>dehumanise</u> the men and reflect the <u>ugliness</u> of their attitudes.

EXAM TIP

Don't forget to include minor characters in your essay...

Dickens knew how to get his message across — even the most minor characters are important to the themes in the novel. Including them in your essay will show off your knowledge and understanding of the text.

Section Three — Characters

Practice Questions

What's your favourite colour? What's your favourite breed of goat? What are your opinions on the current economic climate? All good questions — but thankfully not ones you need to answer. There are some questions you should answer on this page, though. They'll help you consolidate your knowledge, but remember — just write a sentence or so for each question, then power through to the next page.

Quick Questions

1) What is the main thing that Scrooge cares about at the beginning of the novel?

2) Briefly describe Marley's punishment in the afterlife.

3) Write down three features of Fred's personality.

4) Find two examples in the text that show how poor the Cratchit family is.

5) How can you tell that Bob and Tiny Tim have a close relationship?

6) Give an example from the text which shows that Fan cares about Scrooge.

7) Write down two examples from the text which show that Mr Fezziwig is a good boss.

8) Why does Belle break off her engagement with Scrooge?

9) Find a quote that suggests Joe and the thieves are disrespectful towards Scrooge.

10) How do the merchants in Chapter Four react to Scrooge's death?

Practice Questions

Okay, play-time's over... it's time to get serious with some longer questions. Remember to have a think about how you're going to answer each question before you start writing. For the exam-style questions, try to structure your answer as if you were in an exam (there's a handy section on how to do that starting on p.56).

In-depth Questions

1) Describe Scrooge's character at the end of *A Christmas Carol*. Use quotes to back up your answer.

2) Why do you think Marley's appearance is so horrifying?
   Give some examples of things that make him seem scary.

3) Describe the differences between Scrooge and Fred, and explain what effect this has.

4) Explain how Dickens presents Tiny Tim as a good character.

5) Explain the differences between Fezziwig and Scrooge as employers.
   Give some quotes to back up your answer.

6) Why do you think Dickens includes the charity collectors in the novel?

Exam-style Questions

1) Have a look at the passage in Chapter Four which begins with "They scarcely seemed to enter the city" and ends "'But I must be fed, if I make one.'"

   With reference to this passage, discuss how Dickens presents wealthy characters in the novel.
   Write about:
   a) The way the merchants are presented in this passage, and
   b) The way that wealthy characters are presented in the novel as a whole.

2) Read the passage in Chapter Two that starts "But now a knocking at the door was heard," and ends "his sight grew very dim indeed".

   How does Dickens create sympathy for Scrooge in *A Christmas Carol*? You should talk about the above passage in your answer, as well as the rest of the book.

3) Explain the importance of the character of Fred in *A Christmas Carol*.

Section Four — Themes

The Christmas Spirit

The Christmas spirit is everywhere in the novel. These pages are here to show you why it's so darn <u>important</u>.

Christmas brings out the best in people

1) Throughout *A Christmas Carol*, <u>Christmas</u> is presented as a time when people "open their shut-up hearts freely". Several characters in the novel demonstrate this <u>Christmas spirit</u> — they show generosity, charity, kindness and goodwill to others.

2) The <u>Cratchits</u>' Christmas celebration demonstrates their <u>love</u> for each other and their happiness at being <u>together</u>. For example, Bob is <u>disappointed</u> when his wife tells him that Martha isn't coming for Christmas Day, and he's <u>relieved</u> when she appears from her hiding place. It's very important to Bob that the <u>whole family</u> is together for Christmas.

© KINGWILL Marilyn/ArenaPAL

3) Fred fully embraces the <u>spirit</u> of <u>Christmas</u>. He refers to Christmas as a "kind, forgiving, charitable, pleasant time" that brings out the <u>best</u> in people, and he hopes that <u>Scrooge</u> will embrace Christmas too.

> **Character — Ghost of Christmas Present**
>
> The Ghost of Christmas Present, with its "cheery voice" and "joyful air", <u>personifies</u> many of the values associated with Christmas. It's also a symbol of the <u>transforming power</u> of Christmas — it uses its torch to sprinkle <u>incense</u> over anyone who begins to argue, immediately restoring their "<u>good humour</u>".

The Christmas spirit involves generosity and kindness

Many of the <u>characters</u> in the text see Christmas as a time to <u>help</u> those less <u>fortunate</u> than themselves.

1) The <u>charity collectors</u> that visit Scrooge are a good example of this. They refer to Christmas as a time when "<u>Want</u> is keenly felt, and <u>Abundance</u> rejoices". They're trying to provide some festive "Christian cheer" at a time when poverty is made most obvious by the excesses enjoyed by the <u>wealthy</u>.

2) Similarly, <u>Fred</u> believes that Christmas should encourage people "to think of people below them as if they really were <u>fellow-passengers</u> to the grave". He thinks that Christmas is a time when all of <u>humanity</u>, rich and poor, should <u>unite</u> and help each other, rather than carrying on with their business as <u>isolated</u> individuals.

> **Theme — Social Responsibility**
>
> Fred's speech about Christmas in Chapter One is <u>closely linked</u> to the theme of social responsibility. Dickens emphasises the importance of the speech by having Bob <u>applaud</u> it.

3) <u>Fezziwig</u> also demonstrates <u>generosity</u> and <u>kindness</u> of spirit. He has the power to render his apprentices "happy or unhappy", to make their work "light or burdensome; a pleasure or a toil", and chooses to behave in a way that can only bring <u>happiness</u>. He throws a wonderful <u>Christmas party</u> for his employees and exhibits a contagious <u>joy</u> throughout.

> By contrast, Scrooge sees Christmas purely in <u>monetary</u> terms. He questions how Fred can be <u>merry</u> at Christmas when he is "<u>poor</u> enough" — this shows he links happiness with money, even though it doesn't bring him <u>joy</u>. Fred highlights this when he says "His wealth is of <u>no use</u> to him".

The Christmas Spirit

The Christmas spirit has both a religious and a secular side

1) A lot of what Dickens says about the Christmas spirit is related to his view of <u>Christianity</u>. For example, the values that Fred associates with Christmas (kindness, forgiveness and charity) are exactly the kinds of "<u>Christian cheer</u>" that Dickens associated with Christianity — he thought <u>helping others</u> should be an important part of people's <u>faith</u>.

For more about religion and Christmas, see p.9.

2) However, for Dickens, Christmas also had a <u>secular</u> element — there's plenty of evidence of a <u>non-religious</u> celebration of Christmas. As Fred says, Christmas is "a good time", even "apart from the veneration due to its sacred name and origin".

3) A good example of the more secular celebration of Christmas is the childish <u>excitement</u> that surrounds it — particularly at <u>Fred's house</u>, where the family roar with laughter amidst music and games, and at <u>Fezziwig's party</u>. There are similar scenes at the <u>Cratchit home</u>, where the family delight in their small feast and shared companionship.

© Moviestore/REX

4) Dickens links this giddy, <u>childish</u> behaviour back to the religious side of Christmas by saying it's "good to be children sometimes", especially at Christmas, when "its mighty <u>Founder</u> was a child himself".

The Christmas spirit is powerful enough to transform Scrooge

1) At first, Scrooge's reaction to Christmas is "<u>Humbug</u>", and he thinks that anyone who celebrates Christmas is an "<u>idiot</u>".

2) Scrooge's attitude is ridiculed at Fred's party, and he's the only source of <u>anger</u> during the Cratchits' celebrations — he's referred to as the "<u>Ogre</u> of the family" and his name casts "a dark <u>shadow</u>" on the party.

3) By the end of the story, Scrooge is <u>transformed</u> by what he's learned about the Christmas spirit. He wishes everyone he meets a "merry Christmas", he makes a large <u>donation</u> to charity, he <u>buys</u> a huge turkey for the Cratchits, and he even attends his nephew's Christmas <u>party</u>.

4) Scrooge promises to "<u>honour</u> Christmas" in his heart and to "try to keep it <u>all the year</u>".

> Dickens uses *A Christmas Carol* to suggest that the spirit of Christmas is important <u>all year round</u>:
> - The Ghost of Christmas Past carries <u>winter holly</u>, but wears a dress "trimmed with <u>summer flowers</u>". This could suggest that the spirit's lessons should be observed all year round, not just at Christmas.
> - The presence of the two children, <u>Ignorance</u> and <u>Want</u>, in the robes of the Ghost of Christmas Present are a <u>reminder</u> that these problems will still exist once Christmas is over, and that people should <u>remember</u> those less fortunate than themselves at all times — not just at Christmas.

Remember to work context into your answer...

You need to be able to link all that context stuff from Section One with evidence from the text. For example, there's a lovely link just waiting to be made between the Christmas spirit and Dickens's religious views.

Redemption

Understanding Scrooge's redemption is essential in your quest for exam success. The hope that Scrooge will be redeemed is the reason we keep reading. It's Dickens's crafty way of getting us hooked. Sneaky...

Scrooge's redemption is the main focus of the text

1) For Scrooge to achieve <u>redemption</u> he needs to <u>give up</u> his mean and miserly ways, and make up for the bad things he's done. The question of whether or not Scrooge will achieve redemption is a significant source of <u>dramatic tension</u> throughout *A Christmas Carol*.

2) At first, it seems <u>impossible</u> that Scrooge will change. In Chapter One, he's <u>negatively</u> portrayed as a <u>misanthropist</u> whose dislike of other people is shown by his attitude to charity — "It's enough for a man to understand his own business, and not to interfere with other people's".

> A 'misanthropist' is someone who dislikes and distrusts other people.

3) By the time Scrooge is visited by the last ghost, his attitude has softened, and he wants to change his ways, but he's concerned that he's "<u>past all hope</u>". Despite this, Scrooge keeps his <u>promise</u> to change for the better and starts to <u>set things right</u> in the final chapter.

4) <u>Dickens</u> is arguing that even the very <u>worst</u> people in society can find <u>redemption</u>. To do this, they must make the <u>choice</u> to start changing their ways — Marley admits that his chains were forged of his own "free will" because he <u>chose</u> not to change his miserly ways when he was alive.

Theme — Social Responsibility

Although Scrooge is <u>haunted</u> by ghosts, it's the harsh <u>reality</u> of the visions shown to him by the spirits that provide an incentive for him to change, and not a fear of the supernatural. Dickens wants the whole of <u>Victorian society</u> to undergo the same <u>transformation</u> as Scrooge and start to take <u>responsibility</u> for less fortunate people.

There are hints that Scrooge will be redeemed

1) The visions Scrooge sees with the Ghost of Christmas Past show the reader that Scrooge wasn't always so <u>mean-spirited</u>.

2) The visions give the reader an insight into Scrooge's close relationship with <u>Fan</u> and the sad ending of his engagement to <u>Belle</u>. These relationships show that Scrooge is capable of showing <u>love</u> and <u>kindness</u>, and suggest that he can show them <u>again</u>. They also prove that things like love and companionship were once <u>more important</u> to Scrooge than money, and they might become so again.

© Everett Collection/REX

3) Another <u>hint</u> is the change in <u>Scrooge's father</u>, which <u>foreshadows</u> Scrooge's own redemption. Dickens suggests that Scrooge's father was a harsh man who <u>abandoned</u> his son at boarding-school over the Christmas holidays. However, when Fan comes to collect Scrooge, she tells him how their father "is so much <u>kinder</u> than he used to be".

4) Finally, <u>Marley</u> — who's portrayed as being very <u>similar</u> to Scrooge — claims that he's <u>responsible</u> for "procuring" the "chance and hope" that will help Scrooge to save himself (the visits from the three spirits). The fact that Marley is now prepared to help another person, makes it seem <u>more likely</u> that Scrooge will be able to change.

Redemption

Scrooge's changed behaviour leads to his redemption

1) Scrooge's <u>redemption</u> doesn't rely on a <u>religious</u> conversion or him going to church and praying more frequently. Instead, he's redeemed because he changes his <u>behaviour</u> towards other people.

2) This is consistent with Dickens's views on religion (see p.9) — he thought that <u>Christianity</u> should be about <u>practical kindness</u> and willingness to <u>help</u> other people.

3) By the end of the story, Scrooge is "glowing with his good intentions". It's this <u>kindness</u> and <u>generosity</u> that allows him to <u>change</u> his fate and "sponge away" his name from his neglected gravestone. It's as if he's <u>reborn</u>, and he has a second chance to do things better — he even says, "I'm quite a baby".

Scrooge isn't forced to change...

© Alastair Muir/REX

1) The spirits that initiate Scrooge's redemption are sent to <u>help</u> him. They don't force him to change or tell him what to do — they merely <u>show</u> him visions. It's <u>Scrooge</u> himself who must take the meaning from these visions and use that to <u>change</u>.

2) Scrooge is able to redeem himself because he chooses to <u>learn</u> from what these spirits have <u>shown</u> him — he's determined not to "shut out the lessons that they teach".

3) These lessons lead Scrooge to the realisation that "the <u>Time</u> before him was his <u>own</u>, to make <u>amends</u> in" — he can use the rest of his life to make up for his previous behaviour. The fact that Scrooge's transformation is done of his own <u>free will</u> makes his redemption seem more <u>powerful</u>.

... he's transformed by learning the value of empathy

1) At the start of *A Christmas Carol*, Scrooge is used to "warning all human <u>sympathy</u> to keep its <u>distance</u>". However, the spirits' visions teach him how to <u>empathise</u> with other people.

- He feels <u>pity</u> for his lonely, boyhood self and <u>regrets</u> his treatment of the carol singer in Chapter One.

- He remembers the <u>fun</u> that he had as Fezziwig's apprentice and <u>empathises</u> with his own clerk, Bob.

- He <u>learns</u> from the example of his nephew, Fred, who frequently displays <u>empathy</u> — Fred <u>pities</u> his uncle "whether he likes it or not", and he's "heartily sorry" for the death of Tiny Tim.

- He's terrified and disgusted by other people's <u>indifference</u> towards him in his own <u>death</u> — as shown to him by the Ghost of Christmas Yet to Come.

2) Perhaps the most <u>important</u> example of empathy occurs when Scrooge witnesses the <u>love</u> between the <u>Cratchits</u> and feels "an <u>interest</u> he had never felt before" when he asks if Tiny Tim will live. Scrooge's empathy for Tiny Tim is <u>key</u> to his <u>redemption</u> and saves Tim's life.

"I will not shut out the lessons that they teach"

All Scrooge has to do to be redeemed is make a choice. It's as simple as that. Well... he gets a bit of help from the ghosts, but there's no-one poking him with a stick and forcing him to do things differently.

Poverty and Social Responsibility

It's quite a simple message really — people just need to give two hoots about helping the poor.
Don't forget to take a look back at Section One for more on this dazzling piece of Dickensian wisdom.

At first, Scrooge only cares about himself and money

1) Scrooge is <u>apathetic</u> about the plight of the poor. He believes that his <u>taxes</u> pay for the <u>prisons</u> and <u>workhouses</u>, so he doesn't feel he needs to donate anything to charity. He suggests that if they would rather <u>die</u>, "they had better do it" and "decrease the <u>surplus population</u>".

If someone is 'apathetic', they show a lack of interest or concern.

2) Scrooge's views lead him to <u>exploit</u> people like Bob Cratchit. He makes Bob work for low pay and in freezing conditions.

Dickens's <u>childhood experience</u> of poverty (see p.6) influenced him, and he worked <u>very hard</u> to get financial security. Scrooge's fear of poverty <u>echoes</u> Dickens's own concerns about money.

3) Belle explains that Scrooge lives in <u>fear</u> of poverty. He has become engrossed by "the master-passion, <u>Gain</u>" in the hope of being beyond the "<u>sordid reproach</u>" of poverty. Scrooge even remarks of the world, "there is nothing on which it is so <u>hard</u> as poverty".

4) By revealing Scrooge's fear of poverty, Dickens makes Scrooge's attitude to the poor in Chapter One seem <u>even worse</u>. Scrooge knows that poverty is awful, but his fear has made him <u>selfish</u> towards those in need.

Dickens exposes the unfair treatment of the poor

1) Dickens says that some of the chained phantoms in Chapter One might be "<u>guilty governments</u>". This could be seen as a <u>criticism</u> by Dickens of the government's treatment of the poor, e.g. the <u>1834 Poor Law</u>. The chains these ghosts wear are the same as Marley's — they're the result of an <u>uncaring</u> attitude towards the poor.

For more on Dickens's reaction to society's treatment of the poor, see Section One.

2) Dickens uses the <u>Ghost of Christmas Present</u> to condemn the "bigotry, and selfishness" of those who supported <u>Sabbatarianism</u>. Dickens attacks Sabbatarianism because of the <u>restrictions</u> it places on the poor (see p.9).

3) The Ghost of Christmas Present also reveals <u>Ignorance</u> and <u>Want</u> — children who are described as "horrible" monsters. The spirit suggests that these hidden problems are a product of <u>society's neglect</u> of the poor.

The wealthy must take responsibility for the poor

1) The <u>Ghost of Christmas Present</u> gives a clear <u>warning</u> — he says that ignorance will lead to the "Doom" of society. Dickens is pointing out that to <u>avoid</u> this, society must address the lack of <u>education</u> received by the poor.

2) The fate of Tiny Tim makes a clear <u>link</u> between <u>poverty</u> and <u>death</u> — it's only Scrooge's intervention that saves him. Dickens is clearly showing that the wealthy have a <u>responsibility</u> to help the poor because they can make a big difference to their lives.

3) Dickens's message can also be found in the words of Marley when he explains to Scrooge that he must take <u>responsibility</u> for those around him — his true "<u>business</u>" is the "<u>common welfare</u>" of mankind. It's this lesson — of "charity, mercy, forbearance and benevolence" — that Scrooge eventually <u>learns</u>.

Poverty and Social Responsibility

The Cratchits show what living in poverty can be like

1) <u>Dickens</u> uses the <u>Cratchits</u> as an example of people living in poverty.

2) The Cratchits live in a <u>four-room</u> house. Their clothes are <u>threadbare</u>, but they make an effort — Belinda and Mrs Cratchit are "brave in ribbons" and Peter feels "gallantly attired" in his handed-down "shirt collar".

3) The Cratchits' Christmas dinner has to be "<u>Eked out</u>", and their Christmas pudding is "<u>small</u>" for such a large family. Their <u>modest</u> Christmas dinner suggests that they don't have much to eat for the <u>rest of the year</u>.

© Moviestore/REX

4) The Ghost of Christmas Present hints that "if these shadows remain <u>unaltered</u>" — if the Cratchits continue to live in <u>poverty</u> — then Tiny Tim will <u>die</u>. It's only because Scrooge intervenes that Tim survives.

There are also glimpses of the seedier side of poverty

1) Joe's shop — where Scrooge's <u>stolen</u> possessions are sold in Chapter Four — is in a <u>filthy</u> part of the city where the streets are "foul and narrow" and the alleys "like so many cesspools, disgorged their offences of smell, and dirt".

2) The <u>people</u> who live there are "half-naked, drunken, slipshod, ugly".

3) Three thieves gather there to sell the property they've <u>stolen</u> from Scrooge's corpse. They're <u>not embarrassed</u> or <u>remorseful</u>, and they laugh as they go through the stolen goods.

> **Background and Context**
>
> The description of the area where Joe's shop is located gives an insight into the horrible <u>conditions</u> in <u>nineteenth-century London</u> that many people lived in.

Dickens goes beyond simple definitions of rich and poor

1) Dickens shows that while people can be rich <u>financially</u>, they can also be rich in <u>other ways</u>, such as enjoyment, love and companionship.

2) The Cratchits are <u>poor</u> but they <u>appreciate</u> what they have. They're portrayed as an <u>unrealistically</u> perfect family who don't need money to make them <u>emotionally</u> rich. By contrast, Scrooge is <u>financially</u> wealthy, but he's <u>poor</u> in companionship and enjoyment. Fred explains that, even though Scrooge is rich, he's deserving of <u>pity</u> because "His wealth is of no use to him".

3) <u>Fred</u> emphasises the value of emotional richness to him when he says that although <u>Christmas</u> never put "a scrap of gold or silver" in his pocket, it's made him richer in <u>spirit</u> and "done me good".

4) Fezziwig is a <u>successful</u> businessman, but he's also rich <u>emotionally</u>. He uses some of his wealth to bring <u>happiness</u> and <u>joy</u> to himself and those around him.

"This boy is Ignorance. This girl is Want."

Dickens had personal experience of poverty (see p.6), and he was pretty peeved about the way society appeared not to care about the poor. He really hammers the point home in this book. Look at him go...

Family

Happiness and family are inseparable in the novel. That's why Scrooge is so mean and horrible. He's alone.

Dickens highlights the importance of family

1) <u>Family</u> is shown to be a source of comfort, strength and joy throughout the text.

2) Several examples of this can be found in the visions shown to Scrooge by the <u>Ghost of Christmas Present</u> — children "running out into the snow" to greet "sisters, brothers, cousins, uncles, aunts", the "<u>cheerful</u> company" of a miner's family, and a <u>companionable</u> group of sailors, each one comforting himself with thoughts of "those he <u>cared</u> for".

3) The Cratchit family are symbolic of a <u>perfect family</u>. They're very <u>close</u>, and they enjoy affectionately teasing and talking with each other. They're also <u>supportive</u> and <u>loyal</u> — they unite in their <u>grief</u> over Tiny Tim's death.

4) Dickens emphasises that there's <u>nothing special</u> about the Cratchits ("nothing of high mark"), but their family love strengthens them and makes them <u>happy</u>.

> **Background and Context**
>
> In the middle of the nineteenth century, <u>large</u> families were <u>very common</u>. Many families had five or six children — the Cratchits have six.

Family life is shown to be full of happiness

1) Throughout *A Christmas Carol*, Dickens links the theme of <u>family</u> with the idea of <u>happiness</u>. For example, <u>Fred's family</u> are shown having <u>fun</u> together as they celebrate Christmas. Fred's <u>laughter</u> is "irresistibly contagious". His wife "laughed as heartily as he" and their friends "roared out, lustily".

2) Scrooge is also shown a vision of Belle's <u>boisterous</u> and <u>playful</u> family. Belle and her daughter laugh "heartily" at the turmoil caused by the younger children, and Dickens says the family is full of "joy, and gratitude, and ecstasy".

© Moviestore Collection/REX

At first Scrooge doesn't see the point in family

1) In <u>contrast</u> to the other main characters in the text, Scrooge doesn't see the <u>virtue</u> in family life. Every year he <u>dismisses</u> Fred's invitation to dine with his family in favour of solitude.

2) When Fred tells Scrooge that he married because he fell in <u>love</u>, Scrooge <u>laughs</u> at him and says that love is the "one thing in the world more <u>ridiculous</u> than a merry Christmas".

3) <u>Scrooge</u> can only think about the <u>financial burden</u> that <u>family</u> brings. He wonders how Bob Cratchit can feel "<u>merry</u>" at Christmas when he has to <u>support</u> his whole family with his low <u>wage</u> — "my clerk, with fifteen shillings a-week, and a wife and family, talking about a merry Christmas." Similarly, his reaction to the Ghost of Christmas Present's eighteen hundred brothers is to mutter that it's "a tremendous family to <u>provide</u> for".

Family

Scrooge is isolated and alone...

1) In his <u>youth</u>, Scrooge was "a <u>solitary</u> child, neglected by his friends". He weeps when he's shown a vision of himself "<u>alone</u> again" in the "long, bare, melancholy" schoolroom. Scrooge had to create <u>companionship</u> for himself out of the characters in his books to replace his own <u>absent</u> family.

> Dickens suggests that Scrooge had a close relationship with his sister <u>Fan</u>. Her <u>death</u> would have affected him greatly and increased his <u>isolation</u>.

2) This scene <u>foreshadows</u> Scrooge's solitary life later on, after his <u>failure</u> to create a family with <u>Belle</u>. This episode with Belle appears to be a <u>turning point</u> for Scrooge — he stops caring about <u>other people</u> and becomes even more obsessed with <u>money</u>. Scrooge argues that his fixation on money is due to him becoming "wiser", but it's the cause of his <u>loneliness</u>.

> Scrooge's <u>corpse</u> is left "plundered and bereft, unwatched, unwept, uncared for". This contrasts with the <u>tears</u> the Cratchit family shed over the death of <u>Tiny Tim</u>.

3) In Chapter Four, Scrooge sees the result of his <u>rejection</u> of family and the <u>isolation</u> this brings him. After Scrooge's <u>death</u>, one of the thieves says that if the "wicked old screw" had been more "<u>natural</u>" in life, he might have had someone to <u>look after</u> him in death. Scrooge's <u>selfishness</u> means he has <u>no-one</u> to take care of him after he dies.

... but there's still time for Scrooge to become part of a family

1) When Scrooge was a child, he was <u>rescued</u> from his isolation when his <u>father</u> changed and became kinder. When Fan collects Scrooge, she says that the family home is "like Heaven".

> **Background and Context**
>
> Queen Victoria and her husband, Albert, had nine <u>children</u>. Victoria's family was presented as a loving, happy, <u>model family</u> to her subjects.

2) Without a <u>family</u> of his own, Scrooge can't be saved from <u>loneliness</u> in the "haggard winter of his life". He regrets that he missed his chance to have a family with Belle and will now never have a <u>child</u> to call him father.

3) However, at the end, Scrooge becomes a part of two families. He becomes a "<u>second father</u>" to Tiny Tim and endeavours to <u>help</u> the struggling Cratchits. He also embraces his <u>relationship</u> with Fred, and visits him on Christmas day.

> **Character — Marley**
>
> In Chapter One, Marley is presented as the nearest thing to <u>family</u> that Scrooge has — especially since Scrooge chooses not to be part of <u>Fred's family</u>. Scrooge <u>answers</u> to both his own and his partner's name, and Marley passes down his rooms to Scrooge like a family <u>heirloom</u>. As a ghost, Marley shows a deep <u>interest</u> in Scrooge — he's watched over him for years — and it's appropriate that he helps to bring about Scrooge's <u>redemption</u>.

© Alastair Muir/REX

Write about how family is used to create contrasts...

At first, there's a big contrast between happy families like the Cratchits and Scrooge's isolation. But a few ghostly visits later, he's all pally with Fred, and he's got himself a son... sort of. That's some transformation...

Practice Questions

And now for some questions. There are a few quick questions to ease you in gently, and then you've got a selection of in-depth questions to check you've really got to grips with the themes covered in this section.

Quick Questions

1) Give two examples of generous characters in the novel.

2) Write down an example of an occasion when Scrooge feels empathy.

3) Why does Belle think that Scrooge has become obsessed with money?

4) What evidence is there that Scrooge has become part of a family by the end of the novel? Give two examples from the text.

In-depth Questions

1) To what extent do you think Christmas is presented as a religious celebration in the novel? Use evidence from the text in your answer.

2) Do you think it seems likely in the first two chapters that Scrooge will be redeemed by the end of the novel? Explain your answer using evidence from the text.

3) To what extent are the ghosts responsible for Scrooge's transformation? Explain you answer.

4) Aside from having financial wealth, how are characters shown to be rich in the novel?

5) How does Dickens use the visions of the Ghost of Christmas Past to show the importance of family? Use evidence from the text in your answer.

Practice Questions

Themes often come up in exams, so it's vital you know how to write about them. You can practise with these exam-style questions that are conveniently here for you. I know, I know, I really am rather lovely aren't I...

Exam-style Questions

1) Using the extract below as a starting point, explain how Dickens presents the power of the Christmas spirit in *A Christmas Carol*.

Taken from 'Chapter One: Marley's Ghost'

"Don't be cross, uncle," said the nephew.

"What else can I be," returned the uncle, "when I live in such a world of fools as this? Merry Christmas! Out upon merry Christmas! What's Christmas time to you but a time for paying bills without money; a time for finding yourself a year older, and not an hour richer; a time for balancing your books and having every item in 'em through a round dozen of months presented dead against you? If I could work my will," said Scrooge indignantly, "every idiot who goes about with "Merry Christmas" on his lips, should be boiled with his own pudding, and buried with a stake of holly through his heart. He should!"

"Uncle!" pleaded the nephew.

"Nephew!" returned the uncle sternly, "keep Christmas in your own way, and let me keep it in mine."

"Keep it!" repeated Scrooge's nephew. "But you don't keep it."

"Let me leave it alone, then," said Scrooge. "Much good may it do you! Much good it has ever done you!"

"There are many things from which I might have derived good, by which I have not profited, I dare say," returned the nephew. "Christmas among the rest. But I am sure I have always thought of Christmas time, when it has come round — apart from the veneration due to its sacred name and origin, if anything belonging to it can be apart from that — as a good time; a kind, forgiving, charitable, pleasant time; the only time I know of, in the long calendar of the year, when men and women seem by one consent to open their shut-up hearts freely, and to think of people below them as if they really were fellow-passengers to the grave, and not another race of creatures bound on other journeys. And therefore, uncle, though it has never put a scrap of gold or silver in my pocket, I believe that it *has* done me good, and *will* do me good; and I say, God bless it!"

---

2) How does Dickens show the importance of empathy in Scrooge's redemption?

3) How does Dickens explore the idea of social responsibility in *A Christmas Carol*?

4) How does Dickens present poverty in *A Christmas Carol*?

5) How does Dickens use *A Christmas Carol* to explore ideas about family?

Structure and Narrative

The structure of *A Christmas Carol* is simple but effective. The narrator on the other hand, well he's pretty crafty — lulling you into a false sense of security before hitting you with the sympathy vote. Tut tut...

The novel has a simple structure

1) *A Christmas Carol* is divided into <u>five chapters</u>, and Dickens called each chapter a '<u>stave</u>'. Staves are the five lines on which <u>musical notes</u> are written, which may explain why there are <u>five chapters</u>. The word 'stave' is also another word for a <u>verse</u> of a song.

2) The use of <u>staves</u> and the <u>title</u>, *A Christmas Carol*, suggest that this novel, like a <u>carol</u>, was meant to be <u>listened</u> to and enjoyed by groups of people. Reading <u>aloud</u> to friends and family was more <u>common</u> in Victorian times than it is today.

3) Each chapter of the novel has a clear and separate <u>purpose</u>:

- The <u>first chapter</u> introduces Scrooge and emphasises his <u>character flaws</u>, before setting into motion the events that will lead to his <u>redemption</u>.

- The <u>middle three chapters</u> each relate to Scrooge's past, present and future, and they contain various <u>lessons</u> for Scrooge to learn from the three <u>ghosts</u>. The appearance of each ghost is signalled by the ominous tolling of a <u>bell</u>.

- The final chapter <u>reintroduces</u> things from the first chapter, such as the charity collectors. This gives the story a <u>circular structure</u> that clearly shows how Scrooge has <u>changed</u> — Scrooge shows that he's <u>learnt</u> from his experience, saying that he <u>promises</u> to "live in the Past, the Present and the Future".

4) Dickens includes several hints that the story will have a <u>happy ending</u>:

- Scrooge's <u>transformation</u> is foreshadowed by the change in <u>Scrooge's father</u>. The fact that Scrooge was more kind-hearted in his <u>youth</u> also acts as a hint that he will be able to change back.

- In the first few pages of the novel, Dickens uses the phrase "<u>Once upon a time</u>", which links the story to a <u>fairy tale</u> and suggests that it will have a <u>happy ending</u>.

> *Foreshadowing is when a writer gives the reader clues about what will happen later on.*

The story has an unusual time scheme

1) The story doesn't follow a <u>chronological</u> structure. It's mainly set in <u>Scrooge's present</u>, but it includes three <u>separate</u> episodes that have visions set in different time periods — Scrooge's past, present and future.

2) Each individual episode with the ghosts doesn't follow a <u>regular time scheme</u> — each one contains several jumps in time.

3) The <u>linking sections</u> between each ghostly visit are set in <u>Scrooge's present</u>, but they also don't follow the normal rules of time. Scrooge falls asleep after 2 am, but he's visited by the first ghost at 1 am that same night. The tolling of the <u>bell</u> shows that hours are passing, but the three visits only take <u>one night</u>.

Structure and Narrative

Supernatural visits drive the action

1) The reader is repeatedly made aware that the ghosts have a short amount of <u>time</u> to convey their messages to Scrooge. This <u>drives</u> the plot forward and creates dramatic <u>tension</u> that builds with each ghostly visit.

2) The Ghost of Christmas Past <u>instructs</u> Scrooge to "Rise! and walk with me!", and its manner gets more <u>urgent</u> from then on. It tells Scrooge "Let us go on", "Let us see another Christmas!" and, "My <u>time</u> grows short... Quick!"

3) The Ghost of Christmas Present's visit is a blur of <u>activity</u>. Scrooge and the spirit <u>speed</u> through several Christmas visions, but there's a sense that there's barely enough <u>time</u> for Scrooge to learn all that he needs to learn before the spirit leaves — the spirit warns Scrooge "My life upon this globe, is very <u>brief</u>".

4) The Ghost of Christmas Yet to Come is in such a <u>hurry</u> it appears in the chapter of the <u>previous</u> ghost. It rushes Scrooge towards what seems to be his <u>final lesson</u> — the vision of Scrooge's own <u>corpse</u>. Scrooge slows down the <u>pace</u> by <u>refusing</u> to look at the corpse, which increases the <u>tension</u> as the reader worries that Scrooge may run out of time to fully learn his lesson. However, later on, the pace builds as the spirit <u>relentlessly</u> points Scrooge towards his final lesson in the graveyard.

Character — Scrooge

In Chapter Four, Scrooge also has a <u>sense of urgency</u>. He asks the spirit to "Lead on!" and calls his time with the ghost <u>"precious"</u>. This drives the plot forward, but it also shows Scrooge's <u>changed</u> attitude — he's not reluctant to accompany the ghosts any more, because he <u>wants</u> to learn what they have to show him.

The omniscient narrator influences the reader's view of Scrooge

1) The narrator puts the reader at ease immediately with his <u>casual</u> tone and <u>humorous</u> ramblings about the phrase "dead as a doornail". The narrator comes across as a talkative, witty storyteller — Dickens presents the narrator in this way so that the reader <u>likes</u> and <u>trusts</u> him.

2) Once the narrator has the reader's trust, he gives lots of <u>negative opinions</u> about Scrooge, e.g. describing him as a "covetous old <u>sinner</u>" with "ferret eyes". By doing this, Dickens uses the narrator to encourage the reader to <u>despise</u> Scrooge at first.

3) As the novel goes on and Scrooge begins to change, the narrator reveals the feelings and <u>emotions</u> Scrooge is experiencing, causing the reader to <u>sympathise</u> with Scrooge. This allows the narrator to drastically <u>change</u> the reader's opinion of Scrooge over the course of the text, making his eventual transformation even more <u>powerful</u>.

The <u>narrator</u> also shares some of his <u>own</u> feelings and <u>emotions</u> with the reader. For example, he shows a <u>mischievous</u> side to his nature when he talks about Belle's daughter being harassed by her siblings — "What would I not have given to be one of them!" Dickens gives the narrator a light-hearted <u>personality</u> to make him more <u>engaging</u> for the reader.

Write about the effect of the narrator on the reader...

It'll really impress the examiner if, rather than just writing about your reaction to the novel, you write about <u>how</u> Dickens makes you feel a certain way. Hint: it's got a lot to do with that crafty 'omniscient' narrator...

Language

Dickens uses loads of interesting language techniques in the novel, and it's important that you can recognise and write about them. See if you can get your head round a few on these pages. The key is in the detail...

The narrator's language controls the tone

For more on narrative, see p.47.

1) At first, the narrator's chatty language creates a <u>lively</u> and <u>engaging</u> tone — he <u>describes</u> Scrooge's house as looking out of place, as if it had got lost whilst "playing at hide-and-seek with other houses".

> *A Christmas Carol* was written to be read <u>aloud</u> and the narrator's <u>chatty</u> style is perfect for this as it gives the impression of a friendly <u>storyteller</u>.

2) The narrator is also <u>sarcastic</u> — he refers to Scrooge as an "<u>excellent</u> man of business" on the day of Marley's funeral, which he arranged for an "<u>undoubted</u> bargain".

3) However, as the story progresses, the narrator's tone becomes more <u>melancholy</u> — Scrooge's <u>school yard</u> is described as being so <u>silent</u>, that there wasn't even "a sigh among the leafless boughs of one despondent poplar".

4) By Chapter Four, the <u>sarcasm</u> also becomes <u>darker</u> in tone — the desolate graveyard where Scrooge is buried is described as "A <u>worthy</u> place!"

5) In the final chapter, the narrator is <u>lighthearted</u> again making the overall <u>mood</u> of the story joyful and uplifting. The chapter is full of <u>exclamations</u> like "Dear heart alive" and "Oh, glorious, glorious!"

Personification adds to the text's mood

> *'Personification' is when an inanimate object is given human qualities.*

1) Dickens uses <u>personification</u> to bring the novel's settings to life — a "<u>gruff</u> old bell" is described as "peeping <u>slily</u>" down at Scrooge. Later, the onions in the grocers' shops appear "ruddy, brown-faced, broad-girthed" as they sit "<u>winking</u> from their shelves". These playful examples of <u>personification</u> make the city seem exciting and alive, and reflect the energy surrounding Christmas.

2) At other times, <u>personification</u> is used to <u>reinforce</u> what's being described — in the second chapter, the joyful atmosphere is <u>highlighted</u> by the way the "crisp air laughed" as the boys shout to each other.

3) <u>Personification</u> isn't just used to describe <u>objects</u> — it can be used to give human form to <u>abstract concepts</u>. The personification of "Ignorance" and "Want" as ragged, desperate <u>children</u> is a good example of this.

The mood becomes darker to emphasises Dickens's message

The <u>overriding mood</u> of *A Christmas Carol* is jolly and festive. However, Dickens creates a much <u>darker</u> mood when he wants to <u>highlight</u> the message of <u>social responsibility</u> that he's putting across in the novel.

- Marley's <u>appearance</u> is <u>disturbing</u> to focus the reader on the message that he's giving to Scrooge.

- Dickens depicts <u>Ignorance</u> and <u>Want</u> as frightening, miserable children to <u>draw attention</u> to the major problems that he saw in society.

- Dickens powerfully describes the area around <u>Joe's shop</u> to present his reader with a <u>realistic</u>, <u>harsh</u> vision of poverty in London — "the whole quarter reeked with crime, with filth, and misery".

Language

Dickens's descriptions bring the novel to life. They make it easier for you to imagine you're right there with Scrooge and his ghostly visitors. Don't get too lost in the vision though — you've got an exam to prepare for.

Dickens gives clear, vivid descriptions

1) Dickens uses several techniques in his <u>descriptions</u> to help create clear images in the reader's mind and emphasise a particular <u>mood</u> in the text.

- <u>Repeated</u> phrases and <u>lists</u> help to exaggerate the sense of <u>celebration</u> that surrounds Christmas. Each guest at Fezziwig's party is introduced with the phrase "In came". Their attitude as they enter is also shown by a list — "some shyly, some boldly, some gracefully, some awkwardly, some pushing, some pulling". This <u>repetition</u> gives the sense of a <u>bustling</u> room full of lots of people, noise and movement.

- Often <u>long sentences</u> are used to <u>list</u> lots of items — for example in the description of the scene in which the Ghost of Christmas Present first appears. This quickens the <u>pace</u> of the text and creates an atmosphere of <u>excitement</u> — it's as if the narrator is <u>overwhelmed</u> by the abundance he's describing.

- Dickens uses the <u>five senses</u> to make his descriptions <u>vivid</u> and <u>engaging</u>. For example, the scene where the Ghost of Christmas Present appears is brought to life by the "bright <u>gleaming</u> berries", the "<u>delicious</u> steam" coming from the punch, the "<u>roaring</u>" blaze of the fire and the spirit's "cheery <u>voice</u>".

2) The novel also contains vivid <u>negative</u> descriptions, for example:

- The <u>sinister</u> graveyard of Scrooge's future burial is described as "fat with repleted appetite", as if it's gorged on <u>dead bodies</u>.

- Scrooge's old <u>schoolroom</u> is <u>empty</u> and <u>silent</u>, without even "a squeak and scuffle from the mice" or "a drip from the half-thawed water-spout".

© REX

3) Sometimes, Dickens deliberately doesn't describe something to let the reader use their <u>imagination</u>. In Chapter One, he refers to the ghosts' "<u>incoherent</u> sounds of lamentation" and "wailings <u>inexpressibly</u> sorrowful". Dickens's <u>lack of description</u> makes the passage more haunting — it's as if the noise is so awful that it's <u>impossible</u> to describe fully.

Figurative language creates powerful descriptions

1) Dickens uses <u>similes</u> to create a comic and lighthearted <u>mood</u>. Even a <u>sinister</u> image like Marley's chain is <u>softened</u> by a humorous simile — it "wound about him like a tail".

2) However, there are other more <u>sombre</u> examples of figurative language in the text, such as the <u>metaphor</u> used in the description of the fog as being so dense that "the houses opposite were mere phantoms".

3) Dickens often uses <u>hyperbole</u> (exaggeration) to make his descriptions more <u>entertaining</u>. The Cratchits react as if their goose is "the <u>rarest</u> of all birds; a feathered phenomenon, to which a black swan was a matter of course", demonstrating how much they <u>appreciate</u> their meagre Christmas dinner.

KEY QUOTE

"A smell like a washing-day!"

Dickens's descriptions are an assault on the senses — by describing the smells, tastes, sounds, sights and feel of different scenes, he brings Victorian London to life and makes the novel entertaining to read.

Language

Yep... we're still talking about language. Keep going though — this stuff will be super useful in your exam.

Dialogue creates different moods

Dickens uses a lot of <u>dialogue</u> in *A Christmas Carol* to reveal various characters' thoughts and feelings. He also describes the speakers' <u>manner</u> and <u>body language</u>.

- <u>Belle</u> speaks "gently", but <u>honestly</u>. Her tears and her <u>caring</u> language reveal that Scrooge was once loved. She tells Scrooge she's leaving him "With a full heart, for the love of him you once were". Belle's soft, sad words make the reader feel <u>sorry</u> for Scrooge that he's lost her love due to his own <u>greed</u>.

- Dickens <u>contrasts</u> the <u>kind-hearted</u> dialogue of the charity collectors with Scrooge's <u>uncaring</u> response. The charity collectors find it "more than usually desirable" to provide some "slight provision for the poor and destitute". Scrooge says that if the poor "would rather die... they had better do it".

- There's a contrast in <u>Cratchits'</u> dialogue as the <u>tone</u> of their conversation <u>changes</u>. Before Tiny Tim's death, their conversations are littered with enthusiastic <u>exclamations</u> like "Hurrah!" and "Lord bless ye!" But afterwards, their language is <u>sombre</u> — their dialogue seems much quieter and hesitant.

Questions help the reader to engage with the text

1) Dickens often uses <u>questions</u> to <u>engage</u> the reader. At the start of the text, the narrator asks, "Scrooge knew he was dead? Of course he did." This gives the impression of a <u>conversation</u> with the reader — it's as if he's answering their questions.

2) The narrator also asks questions and leaves them <u>unanswered</u> — when Scrooge sees people from his childhood celebrating Christmas, the narrator asks "What was merry Christmas to Scrooge?... What good had it ever done to him?" These <u>questions</u> make the reader <u>think</u> about what Scrooge might have been like once.

3) Dickens also uses questions to show how Scrooge is <u>changing</u>:

- The Ghost of Christmas Past tries to get Scrooge to say what he's <u>feeling</u> by asking questions like "<u>What</u> is the matter?" and "Something, I think?" The ghost is trying to draw the <u>emotions</u> out of Scrooge.

- The Ghost of Christmas Present asks Scrooge questions that force him to <u>think</u> about his attitude — "Will you decide what men shall live, what men shall die?" Scrooge also asks questions, which shows his <u>willingness</u> to <u>learn</u> — "Is there a peculiar flavour in what you sprinkle from your torch?"

- The last ghost doesn't speak, so <u>Scrooge</u> is left to ask all the <u>questions</u>. At the end of the chapter, he frantically asks the ghost "Are these the shadows of the things that Will be". He doesn't receive any <u>answers</u>, but his questions <u>reveal</u> that he's determined to <u>change</u> his ways.

4) Although the ghosts' questions are directed at <u>Scrooge</u>, they're also designed to make the <u>reader</u> think about their <u>own</u> attitude, and whether they should take more <u>responsibility</u> for those around them.

EXAM TIP

Show why Dickens's language is important...

It's not enough just to identify a feature of Dickens's language and give an example — you've got to follow it up by developing your point and showing what effect the language has and why Dickens has used it.

Section Five — Writer's Techniques

Symbolism and Imagery

Cymbals are loud percussion instruments that should never be given to children. Oh wait, this page is about symbols... my bad. Symbols are all about hidden meanings. They crop up all the time in *A Christmas Carol*.

Dickens uses symbols to develop his ideas

1) Marley's chain was <u>forged</u> by him "link by link" of his "own <u>free will</u>". The fact that it's made out of cash-boxes, keys, padlocks and ledgers symbolises Marley's obsession with <u>money</u> and how that led him to <u>selfishly</u> ignore his "fellowmen".

2) The children, <u>Ignorance</u> and <u>Want</u>, are clear <u>symbols</u> in the novel. They <u>personify</u> the problems caused by society's <u>neglect</u> of the poor.

3) There are many symbols associated with the <u>ghosts</u>, for example:

> ### Theme — Social Responsibility
> Dickens uses a lot of symbols and imagery to <u>strengthen</u> his <u>message</u> about social responsibility. A <u>powerful</u> symbol or image, like Ignorance and Want, will <u>stay</u> in the reader's head.

- The "bright, clear jet of <u>light</u>" that shines from the Ghost of Christmas Past's head could symbolise the <u>truth</u> that can be found in <u>memories</u>.

- The Ghost of Christmas Present's <u>torch</u>, which it uses to spread good will, is a symbol of the <u>transforming power</u> of Christmas. He also wears a rusty <u>scabbard</u> without a sword, which is a symbol of <u>peace</u>.

- The dark <u>shroud</u> worn by the Ghost of Christmas Yet to Come almost entirely covers it, symbolising that Scrooge's future is <u>ominous</u> and <u>uncertain</u>.

Warmth and brightness symbolise joy and companionship

1) Throughout *A Christmas Carol*, images of <u>fire</u> and <u>brightness</u> are used as symbols of <u>emotional warmth</u>.

2) Several of these images of fire and brightness are shown to Scrooge by the <u>Ghost of Christmas Present</u>. It shows miners "assembled round a <u>glowing</u> fire" and the lighthouse men's fire that throws out a "ray of <u>brightness</u> on the awful sea". All of these images use fire as a symbol of comfort and celebration.

3) This idea is developed further when Scrooge and the spirit travel along the streets, they see the "<u>brightness</u> of the roaring fires" lighting up kitchens and parlours, and the "flickering of the <u>blaze</u>" that reveals preparations for "<u>cosy</u>" dinners. All these <u>joyful</u> scenes take place in the glow of fires.

4) In contrast, Scrooge keeps his rooms <u>dark</u> because "darkness is cheap". He has "a very <u>small</u> fire" in his offices and "a very <u>low</u> fire" at home. The <u>lack</u> of warmth and light in Scrooge's life symbolises his lack of <u>joy</u> and <u>companionship</u>.

© WATERBURY FILMS/CINEMA CENTER FILMS / THE KOBAL COLLECTION / GRYSPEERDT, NORMAN

> At the end, Scrooge tells Bob to "<u>Make up</u> the fires". This is symbolic of Scrooge's <u>transformation</u>, and the fact that he has learnt to understand the importance of showing <u>kindness</u> and <u>generosity</u> to others.

Symbolism and Imagery

Music is an important symbol of celebration and happiness

1) Music is central to the <u>Christmas celebrations</u> at Fezziwig's party and at Fred's house, and Dickens also mentions the <u>singing</u> of Tiny Tim, the miners and the lighthouse men.

2) There's a strong <u>contrast</u> between the joy and happiness of Fred's "musical family" and the lonely, miserable Scrooge, whose life is <u>without music</u> (this is emphasised when Scrooge scares away the <u>carol singer</u> in Chapter One).

3) Music is also shown to have a <u>powerful</u> emotional effect. When Scrooge hears some music performed by his niece (Fred's wife), he wonders whether if he'd been able to listen to it more, "he might have cultivated the kindnesses of life for his own <u>happiness</u> with his <u>own hands</u>". Dickens is arguing that music is so <u>powerful</u> in creating happiness that it could've transformed Scrooge's life.

© Ray Tang/REX

Scrooge's bed is a motif

A motif is a recurring object or idea in a literary work.

1) The first ghost's visit begins at Scrooge's <u>bed</u>, and after the last ghost's visit, he's returned to his bed — when the Ghost of Christmas Past appears it draws back the <u>curtains</u> of Scrooge's bed, whilst the Ghost of Christmas Yet to Come dwindles "down into a <u>bedpost</u>".

2) A person's bed is a <u>private</u> place, so it's important that the ghosts' <u>visits</u> begin and end at Scrooge's bed — they want to access his most private thoughts and emotions. The bed is also a place that is associated with sleeping and <u>dreaming</u> — this emphasises the dreamlike, unreal quality of the visions shown to Scrooge, making it easier for the reader to <u>suspend their disbelief</u>.

Weather reflects Scrooge's character and emotions

1) Throughout the first chapter, Dickens emphasises the <u>fog</u> and <u>cold</u> that surrounds <u>Scrooge</u>. The fog is shown "pouring in at every chink and keyhole", whilst the weather is described as "cold, bleak, biting". The weather is symbolic of Scrooge's <u>cold-hearted isolation</u>.

In Chapter One the <u>fog</u> and <u>frost</u> hangs about Scrooge's house so that it seemed as if "the Genius of the Weather sat in <u>mournful meditation</u> on the threshold". This is an example of <u>pathetic fallacy</u> — when <u>natural</u> elements are given human characteristics to add to a scene's <u>mood</u> or to reflect a character's <u>emotions</u>.

2) Scrooge is described as carrying "<u>cold</u> within him", and his presence "<u>iced</u> his office". Scrooge's <u>cold</u> and <u>bitter</u> personality is presented as being more <u>powerful</u> than the weather — the narrator explains "No warmth could warm, nor wintry weather chill him. No wind that blew was bitterer than he".

3) In the final chapter, the weather becomes a symbol of Scrooge's <u>transformation</u>. The fog has gone, symbolising how Scrooge has had his <u>eyes opened</u> and can clearly <u>see</u> those around him. The weather is "<u>clear</u>, bright, jovial, stirring", and the cold is "piping for the blood to dance to", which represents Scrooge's new <u>brightness</u> and <u>enthusiasm</u> for life.

KEY QUOTE

"He carried his own low temperature always about with him"

Symbols and images are everywhere in the novel. At first, Scrooge is associated with the cold to highlight his bitterness and isolation. By contrast, all of the Christmas revellers in the novel party by nice, toasty fires.

Practice Questions

Surprise, surprise, this chapter finishes with... drum roll please.... some more practice questions. I knew you'd be pleased. Have a go at these quick questions first of all. They're all about the writer's techniques — shocker.

Quick Questions

1) What does 'stave' mean? Give two answers.

2) Give one example of the narrator's chatty style.

3) Find an example of personification in the text.

4) Give an example of a part of the text which has a darker mood.

5) What does Marley's chain symbolise?

6) Give an example of a symbol associated with each one of the ghosts.

7) What does music symbolise in the novel?

8) Find an example of a vivid, negative description in the text.

9) Find an example of a time when Dickens deliberately doesn't fully describe something.

10) Give three examples of similes in the novel.

Practice Questions

These questions are a bit trickier than the ones on the last page — try to write about a paragraph for each. You've also got to make sure you back up what you're saying with quotes and evidence from the text. These questions should really get you thinking about all the different techniques Dickens uses. So let's get started...

In-depth Questions

1) Are there any hints in the first part of the novel that it will have a happy ending? Give some examples from the text.

2) To what extent do you think the novel has an unusual time scheme? Give some examples from the novel to back up your answer.

3) "The ghosts increase the pace of the novel." Do you agree with this statement? Explain your answer.

4) How does the narrator influence the reader's opinion of Scrooge?

5) How does Dickens use dialogue to create a sombre mood among the Cratchits after Tiny Tim's death?

6) Explain how the narrator uses questions to engage the reader.

7) How are warmth and brightness used as symbols in the novel?

8) Explain how the weather and Scrooge are linked in the text.

9) How does Dickens use repetitive language in the novel?

Practice Questions

You're nearly there. Just one more page of exam-style questions before this section is totally done and dusted. These questions are the ones that will really prepare you for the exam. Some of them are tricky little blighters, but if you can get your head round them, it'll make your exam experience a lot less stressful. Give 'em a go...

Exam-style Questions

1) Using the extract below as a starting point, explain the role of the narrator in *A Christmas Carol*.

> Taken from 'Chapter One: Marley's Ghost'
>
> Marley was dead: to begin with. There is no doubt whatever about that. The register of his burial was signed by the clergyman, the clerk, the undertaker, and the chief mourner. Scrooge signed it: and Scrooge's name was good upon 'Change, for anything he chose to put his hand to. Old Marley was as dead as a doornail.
> Mind! I don't mean to say that I know, of my own knowledge, what there is particularly dead about a doornail. I might have been inclined, myself, to regard a coffin-nail as the deadest piece of ironmongery in the trade. But the wisdom of our ancestors is in the simile; and my unhallowed hands shall not disturb it, or the Country's done for. You will therefore permit me to repeat, emphatically, that Marley was as dead as a doornail.
> Scrooge knew he was dead? Of course he did. How could it be otherwise? Scrooge and he were partners for I don't know how many years. Scrooge was his sole executor, his sole administrator, his sole assign, his sole residuary legatee, his sole friend and sole mourner. And even Scrooge was not so dreadfully cut up by the sad event, but that he was an excellent man of business on the very day of the funeral, and solemnized it with an undoubted bargain.
> The mention of Marley's funeral brings me back to the point I started from. There is no doubt that Marley was dead. This must be distinctly understood, or nothing wonderful can come of the story I am going to relate. If we were not perfectly convinced that Hamlet's Father died before the play began, there would be nothing more remarkable in his taking a stroll at night, in an easterly wind, upon his own ramparts, than there would be in any other middle-aged gentleman rashly turning out after dark in a breezy spot—say Saint Paul's Churchyard, for instance — literally to astonish his son's weak mind.

2) How does Dickens create a sense of urgency and tension in Chapters Two, Three and Four?

3) Explore the way the mood changes over the course of the novel.

4) Explore the effects of Dickens's use of symbolism in *A Christmas Carol*.

Exam Preparation

Getting to know the text will put you at a massive advantage in the exam. It's not enough just to read it though — you've got to get down and dirty with the nitty gritty bits. It's all about gathering evidence...

The exam questions will test four main skills

You will need to show the examiner that you can:

1) Write about the text in a <u>thoughtful way</u> — <u>picking out</u> appropriate <u>examples</u> and <u>quotations</u> to back up your opinions.

2) <u>Identify</u> and <u>explain</u> features of the text's <u>form</u>, <u>structure</u> and <u>language</u>. Show how the author uses these to create <u>meanings</u> and <u>effects</u>.

3) Relate the text to its <u>cultural, social and historical background</u>.

4) Write in a <u>clear</u>, <u>well-structured</u> way. <u>5%</u> of the marks in your English Literature exams are for <u>spelling</u>, <u>punctuation</u> and <u>grammar</u>. Make sure that your writing is as <u>accurate</u> as possible.

Preparation is important

1) It's <u>important</u> to cover <u>all</u> the <u>different sections</u> of this book in your <u>revision</u>. You need to make sure you <u>understand</u> the text's <u>context</u>, <u>plot</u>, <u>characters</u>, <u>themes</u> and <u>writer's techniques</u>.

2) In the <u>exam</u>, you'll need to <u>bring together</u> your <u>ideas</u> about these topics to answer the question <u>quickly</u>.

3) Think about the different <u>characters</u> and <u>themes</u> in the text, and write down some <u>key points</u> and <u>ideas</u> about each one. Then, find some <u>evidence</u> to support each point — this could be something from <u>any</u> of the <u>sections</u> in this book. You could set out your evidence in a <u>table</u> like this:

Theme: Poverty and Social Responsibility	
Unfair treatment of poor	Malthus, Poor Laws, workhouses. Scrooge's comments on "surplus population".
Ignorance and Want	Personification of problems in society. "Doom" written on Ignorance's forehead.
Cratchits' poverty	Have little to eat. Hard-working. Can't help Tiny Tim get better.
Seedier side of poverty	Joe's shop. Thieves stealing from Scrooge's corpse. The area "reeked with crime, with filth, and misery".
Scrooge's fear of poverty	Scrooge fears the "sordid reproach" of poverty. Dickens also feared poverty.

Preparing to succeed — a cunning plot indeed...

Knowing the plot inside-out will be unbelievably helpful in the exam. It'll help you to stay calm and make sure you write a brilliant answer that positively glitters with little gems of evidence. The exam's just a chance for you to show off...

The Exam Question

This page deals with how to approach an exam question. The stuff below will help you get started on a <u>scorching exam answer</u>, more scorching than, say, a phoenix cooking fiery fajitas in a flaming furnace.

Read the question carefully and underline key words

1) The style of question you'll get depends on which <u>exam board</u> you're taking.

2) Read all the <u>instructions</u> carefully. Make sure you know <u>how many</u> questions you need to answer and <u>how much time</u> you should spend answering each question.

3) If the question has <u>more than one part</u>, look at the total number of marks for each bit. This should help you to plan your <u>time</u> in the exam.

4) <u>Read</u> the question at least <u>twice</u> so you completely understand it. <u>Underline</u> the key words. If you're given an <u>extract</u>, underline <u>important</u> words or phrases in that too.

Henry didn't read the weather report carefully enough when planning his weekend activities.

Here's an exam-style question

'<u>How</u> questions' ask you to think about the <u>writer's</u> <u>techniques</u>. E.g. Dickens's use of <u>language</u> and <u>imagery</u>.

Remember to write about <u>form</u>, <u>structure</u> and <u>language</u>.

Keep your answer <u>focused</u> on the <u>theme</u> of <u>poverty</u> — but make sure to use a <u>range</u> of <u>examples</u> to support your answer.

Q1 <u>How</u> does Dickens <u>present</u> attitudes towards <u>poverty</u> in the novel?
Refer to the <u>following extract</u> in your answer.

You must <u>refer to</u> and <u>quote from</u> the given extract in your answer.

Some exam boards will ask you to write <u>only</u> about the extract. Others will ask you to write about the extract <u>and</u> the text as a whole. Make sure you read the instructions carefully.

Get to know exam language

Some <u>words</u> come up time and again in <u>exam questions</u>. Have a look at some <u>specimen</u> questions, pick out words that are <u>often used</u> in questions, and make sure you <u>understand</u> what they mean. You could <u>write a few down</u> whilst you're revising. For example:

Question Word	You need to...
Explore / Explain	Show <u>how</u> the writer deals with a <u>theme</u>, <u>character</u> or <u>idea</u>. Make several <u>different</u> points to answer the question.
How does	Think about the <u>techniques</u> or <u>literary features</u> that the author uses to get their point across.
Give Examples	Use <u>direct quotes</u> and describe <u>events</u> from the text in your own words.
Refer to	Read the question so that you know if you need to write about just an <u>extract</u>, or an extract and the <u>rest of the text</u>.

The advice squad — the best cops in the NYPD...

Whatever question you're asked in the exam, your answer should touch on the main characters, themes, structure and language of the text. All the stuff we've covered in the rest of the book in fact. It's so neat, it's almost like we planned it.

Planning Your Answer

I'll say this once — and then I'll probably repeat it several times — it is absolutely, completely, totally and utterly essential that you make a plan before you start writing. Only a fool jumps right in without a plan...

Plan your answer before you start

1) If you plan, you're less likely to forget something important.
2) A good plan will help you organise your ideas — and write a good, well-structured essay.
3) Write your plan at the top of your answer booklet and draw a neat line through it when you've finished.
4) Don't spend too long on your plan. It's only rough work, so you don't need to write in full sentences. Here are a few examples of different ways you can plan your answer:

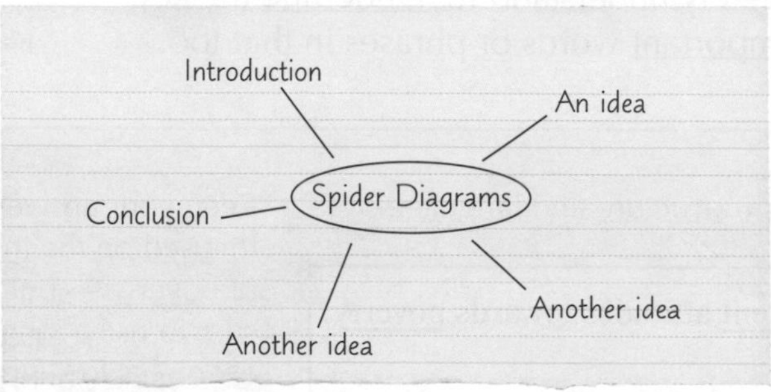

Bullet points...

- Introduction...
- An idea...
- The next idea...
- Another idea...
- Yet another idea...
- Conclusion...

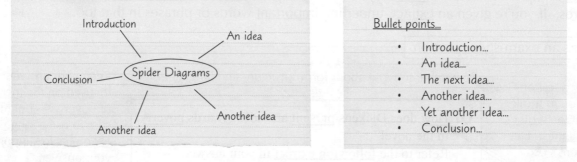

Include bits of evidence in your plan

1) Writing your essay will be much easier if you include important quotes and examples in your plan.
2) You could include them in a table like this one:
3) Don't spend too long writing out quotes though. It's just to make sure you don't forget anything when you write your answer.

A point...	Quote to back this up...
Another point...	Quote...
A different point...	Example...
A brand new point...	Quote...

Structure your answer

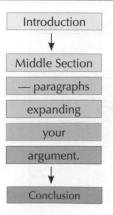

Introduction
↓
Middle Section — paragraphs expanding your argument.
↓
Conclusion

1) Your introduction should give a brief answer to the question you're writing about. Make it clear how you're going to tackle the topic.
2) The middle section of your essay should explain your answer in detail and give evidence to back it up. Write a paragraph for each point you make. Make sure you comment on your evidence and explain how it helps to prove your point.
3) Remember to write a conclusion — a paragraph at the end which sums up your main points. There's more about introductions and conclusions on the next page.

Dirk finally felt ready to tackle the topic.

To plan or not to plan, that is the question...

The answer is yes, yes, a thousand times yes. Often students dive right in, worried that planning will take up valuable time. But 5 minutes spent organising a well-structured answer is loads better than pages of waffle. Mmm waffles.

Writing Introductions and Conclusions

Now you've made that plan that I was banging on about on the last page, you'll know what your main points are. This is going to make writing your introduction and conclusion as easy as pie.

Get to the point straight away in your introduction

1) First, you need to <u>work out</u> what the question is <u>asking you</u> to do:

> How is the character of Bob Cratchit important to *A Christmas Carol*?

> The question is <u>asking you</u> to think about the <u>role</u> of <u>Bob Cratchit</u> in the text.
> Plan your essay by thinking about <u>how</u> this character <u>links</u> to the text's overall <u>message</u>.

2) When you've <u>planned</u> your essay, you should <u>start</u> it by giving a <u>clear answer</u> to the <u>question</u> in a sentence or two. Use the <u>rest</u> of the <u>introduction</u> to <u>develop</u> this idea. Try to include the <u>main paragraph ideas</u> that you have listed in your plan, but <u>save</u> the <u>evidence</u> for later.

3) You could also use the <u>introduction</u> to give your <u>opinion</u>. Whatever you do, make sure your introduction makes it <u>clear</u> how your answer <u>fits the question</u>.

Your conclusion must answer the question

1) The <u>most important</u> thing you have to do at the <u>end</u> of your writing is to <u>summarise</u> your <u>answer</u> to the question.

2) It's your <u>last chance</u> to persuade the examiner, so make your <u>main point</u> again.

3) Use your <u>last sentence</u> to really <u>impress</u> the <u>examiner</u> — it will make your essay <u>stand out</u>. You could <u>develop</u> your own <u>opinion</u> of the text or <u>highlight</u> which of your <u>points</u> you thought was the most <u>interesting</u>.

The examiner was struggling to see the answer clearly.

Use the exact question words in your introduction and conclusion

1) Try to use <u>words</u> or <u>phrases</u> from the <u>question</u> in your introduction and conclusion.

> How does Dickens create the mood of *A Christmas Carol*?

2) This will show the examiner that you're <u>answering the question</u>.

> Dickens creates the mood of the novel largely through the use of an omniscient narrator, who speaks with a lighthearted tone. However, there are other key factors to consider, such as Dickens's use of personification and dialogue.

The first line of the introduction gives a clear answer, which will lead on to the rest of the essay.

3) This will also help you keep the question <u>fresh in your mind</u> so your answer doesn't <u>wander off-topic</u>.

I've come to the conclusion that I really like pie...

To conclude, the introduction eases the examiner in gently, whilst the conclusion is your last chance to impress. But remember — the examiner doesn't want to see any new points lurking in those closing sentences.

Writing Main Paragraphs

So we've covered the beginning and the end, now it's time for the meaty bit. The roast beef in between the prawn cocktail and the treacle tart. This page is about how to structure your paragraphs. It's quite simple...

P.E.E.D. is how to put your argument together

Remember to start a new paragraph every time you make a new point.

1) P.E.E.D. stands for: Point, Example, Explain, Develop.

2) Begin each paragraph by making a point. Then give an example from the text (either a quote or a description). Next, explain how your example backs up your point.

3) Finally, try to develop your point by writing about its effect on the reader, how it links to another part of the text or what the writer's intention is in including it.

Use short quotes to support your ideas

1) Don't just use words from the novel to prove what happens in the plot...

> Marley's ghost wears a chain: "I wear the chain I forged in life".

This just gives an example from the plot without offering any explanation or analysis.

2) Instead, it's much better to use short quotes as evidence to support a point you're making.

3) Also, it makes the essay structure clearer and smoother if most quotes are embedded in your sentences.

It's better to use short, embedded quotes as evidence. Then you can go on to explain them.

> Marley's ghost must wear the chain that he "forged in life" as a punishment for the way he behaved when he was alive. The chain is made from cashboxes, padlocks, ledgers and steel purses, which symbolise Marley's obsession with money.

Get to know some literary language

1) Using literary terms in your answer will make your essay stand out — as long as you use them correctly.

2) When you're revising, think about literary terms that are relevant to the text and how you might include them in an essay. Take a look at the table below for some examples.

Literary Term	Definition	Example
Personification	A figure of speech that talks about a thing as if it's a person.	"the crisp air laughed"
Hyperbole	A way of exaggerating something for emphasis.	"a squeezing, wrenching, grasping, scraping, clutching, covetous, old sinner"
Dramatic Irony	When the reader knows more about a situation than a character.	"The case of this unhappy man might be my own."

This page is so exciting — I nearly...

Now now, let's all be grown ups and avoid the obvious joke. It's a good way of remembering how to structure your paragraphs though. Point, Example, Explain, Develop. Simple. Maybe we could make a rap or something... anyone?

Section Six — Exam Advice

In the Exam

Keeping cool in the exam can be tricky. But if you take in all the stuff on this page, you'll soon have it down to a fine art. Then you can stroll out of that exam hall with the swagger of an essay-writing master.

Don't panic if you make a mistake

1) Okay, so say you've timed the exam beautifully. Instead of putting your feet up on the desk for the last 5 minutes, it's a good idea to <u>read through</u> your <u>answers</u> and <u>correct any mistakes</u>...

2) If you want to get rid of a mistake, <u>cross it out</u>. <u>Don't scribble</u> it out as this can look messy. Make any corrections <u>neatly</u> and <u>clearly</u> instead of writing on top of the words you've already written.

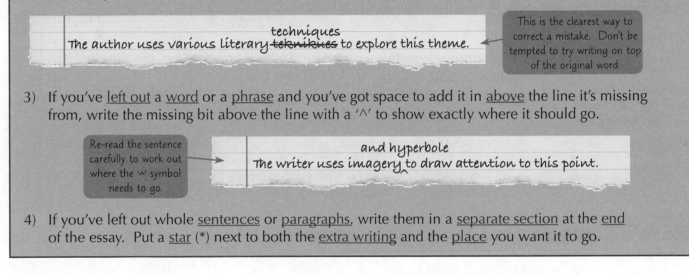

techniques

The author uses various literary ~~teknikues~~ to explore this theme.

This is the clearest way to correct a mistake. Don't be tempted to try writing on top of the original word.

3) If you've <u>left out</u> a <u>word</u> or a <u>phrase</u> and you've got space to add it in <u>above</u> the line it's missing from, write the missing bit above the line with a '^' to show exactly where it should go.

Re-read the sentence carefully to work out where the '^' symbol needs to go.

and hyperbole

The writer uses imagery ^ to draw attention to this point.

4) If you've left out whole <u>sentences</u> or <u>paragraphs</u>, write them in a <u>separate section</u> at the <u>end</u> of the essay. Put a <u>star</u> (*) next to both the <u>extra writing</u> and the <u>place</u> you want it to go.

Always keep an eye on the time

1) It's surprisingly <u>easy</u> to <u>run out of time</u> in exams. You've got to leave <u>enough time</u> to answer <u>all</u> the questions you're asked to do. You've also got to leave enough time to <u>finish</u> each essay properly — with a <u>clear ending</u>.

2) Here are some <u>tips</u> on how to <u>avoid</u> running out of time:

- Work out <u>how much time</u> you have for each part of your answer <u>before</u> you <u>start</u>.
- Take off a few minutes at the beginning to <u>plan</u>, and a <u>few minutes</u> at the end for your <u>conclusion</u>.
- Make sure you have a <u>watch</u> to <u>time yourself</u> — and keep checking it.
- Be <u>strict</u> with yourself — if you spend <u>too long</u> on one part of your answer, you may run out of time.
- If you're <u>running out of time</u>, keep <u>calm</u>, <u>finish</u> the <u>point</u> you're on and move on to your <u>conclusion</u>.

Stephanie never had a problem with keeping cool.

Treat an exam like a spa day — just relax...

Some people actually do lose the plot when they get into the exam. The trick is to keep calm and well... carry on. If you make sure you get your exam technique sorted, you'll be as relaxed as a sloth in a room full of easy chairs.

Section Six — Exam Advice

Sample Exam Question

And now the bit you've all been waiting for — a sample exam question and a lovely little plan.
Go and make yourself a cup of tea, then settle down and enjoy.

Here's a sample exam question...

Read this feisty exam question. That's the best way to start...

In the exam, you'll be given the full extract in the exam paper.

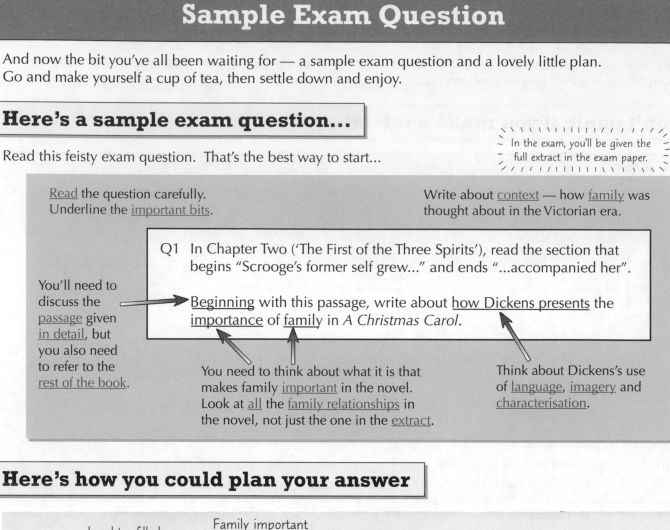

Read the question carefully. Underline the <u>important bits</u>.

Write about <u>context</u> — how <u>family</u> was thought about in the Victorian era.

Q1 In Chapter Two ('The First of the Three Spirits'), read the section that begins "Scrooge's former self grew..." and ends "...accompanied her".

<u>Beginning</u> with this passage, write about <u>how Dickens presents</u> the <u>importance</u> of <u>family</u> in *A Christmas Carol*.

You'll need to discuss the <u>passage</u> given <u>in detail</u>, but you also need to refer to the <u>rest of the book</u>.

You need to think about what it is that makes family <u>important</u> in the novel. Look at <u>all</u> the <u>family relationships</u> in the novel, not just the one in the <u>extract</u>.

Think about Dickens's use of <u>language</u>, <u>imagery</u> and <u>characterisation</u>.

Here's how you could plan your answer

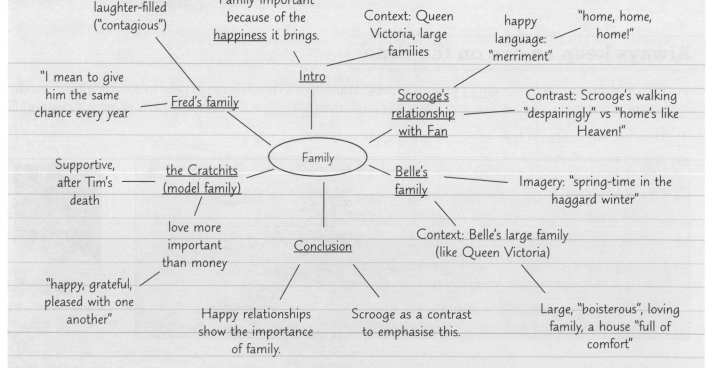

laughter-filled ("contagious")

Family important because of the <u>happiness</u> it brings.

Context: Queen Victoria, large families

happy language: "merriment"

"home, home, home!"

"I mean to give him the same chance every year"

<u>Intro</u>

<u>Fred's family</u>

<u>Scrooge's relationship with Fan</u>

Contrast: Scrooge's walking "despairingly" vs "home's like Heaven!"

Supportive, after Tim's death

<u>the Cratchits (model family)</u>

Family

<u>Belle's family</u>

Imagery: "spring-time in the haggard winter"

love more important than money

<u>Conclusion</u>

Context: Belle's large family (like Queen Victoria)

"happy, grateful, pleased with one another"

Happy relationships show the importance of family.

Scrooge as a contrast to emphasise this.

Large, "boisterous", loving family, a house "full of comfort"

What do examiners eat? Why, egg-sam-wiches of course...

The most important thing to remember is DON'T PANIC. Take a deep breath, read the question, read it again, write a plan... take another deep breath... and start writing. Leave a few minutes at the end to check your answer too.

Worked Answer

This bit will show you how to take an OK answer and turn it into a great one, that will impress the examiner.

Use your introduction to get off to a good start

These pages are all about how to word your sentences to impress the examiner, so we haven't included everything from the plan on page 62.

You might start with something like...

> Dickens presents the importance of family in the novel using a variety of techniques, including imagery and characterisation. Dickens emphasises that families can bring joy and comfort.

1) This intro is okay. It uses some technical terms, to show that the student knows their stuff.

2) It's also a good idea to use the key words from the question to give your essay focus, and to show the examiner you're on track and that you're thinking about the question from the start.

3) But there's still room for improvement...

> In 'A Christmas Carol', Dickens uses a variety of techniques, including imagery, language techniques and characterisation to present the importance of family in leading a happy life. At the time when Dickens was writing, a positive image of family was clearly important as Queen Victoria's own family was presented as a model for a loving and happy family to her subjects. Dickens's favourable portrayal of family and the role it plays in a happy life is strongly contrasted by Scrooge's loneliness — his life without family is presented as miserable and undesirable to the reader.

This intro talks about the social and historical context.

By mentioning the reader, you show you're thinking about what Dickens is trying to tell you.

Develop each point with detailed comments and quotes

> Fan's appearance at Scrooge's school shows the importance of family. Fan has successfully convinced her father to let Scrooge come home to have a merry Christmas with his family, rather than the sad and lonely one he would have had at school.

1) This paragraph makes a point about the extract, and gives some detail about what happens in the scene. But it doesn't develop the point fully, and it doesn't give any quotes as evidence.

2) You should develop your points with evidence and analysis:

> Dickens uses Fan's visit to Scrooge to contrast the misery of isolation with the happiness of family life. When he's alone at the school, Scrooge walks "despairingly", and the room he is in is unpleasant: the windows are "cracked" and there are "fragments of plaster" missing from the ceiling. In contrast, Fan says that their Christmas as a family will be "the merriest time in all the world". Dickens presents spending time with family as a happy event, so Fan's language is very positive. Her speech is full of exclamation marks and repetition to indicate her enthusiastic tone — "To bring you home, home, home!". Fan's joy suggests that families are important because they can be a source of happiness, as well as a way to escape isolation.

This makes a relevant point about the extract, and then goes on to give more detail.

Analysing the characters' language will help you get top marks.

Remember to back up your points with quotes from the novel.

Worked Answer

Link your points to the novel's context and themes

Here's a point you could make about the way that Scrooge represents life without family.

> The character of Scrooge is portrayed as lonely, and he becomes very miserable when he sees his old fiancée's happy family. Dickens is suggesting that having no family can lead to a horrible, sad life.

1) This paragraph builds on the links between a lack of family and loneliness.

2) However, you can improve it by discussing the techniques Dickens uses:

> Elsewhere in the novel, Dickens contrasts Scrooge's loneliness with the happiness of others, using imagery to emphasise the importance of family. In Chapter Two, Scrooge sees a vision of his old fiancée with her family. Scrooge begins to wish he'd had a child, to be "a spring-time in the haggard winter of his life". This metaphor compares Scrooge's life negatively to a dark, bleak "haggard winter", and suggests that having had children would have been "a spring-time to him", bringing joy to his old age. Dickens suggests that being part of a family significantly improves a person's life.

Show that you know the whole novel, not just the extract text.

Don't forget to explain how your points link to the exam question.

3) You could develop this by focusing on the context in which the novel was written:

> Queen Victoria's large family was seen as a model family in the nineteenth century, and both Belle and the Cratchits have large and happy families. Scrooge stands out in the novel as being unusual because he isn't part of a family. However, after his transformation, Scrooge becomes a second father to Tiny Tim, and he engages with Fred's family. Being part of a family is a key part of his new-found happiness.

The examiner will be impressed if you can link the text to the novel's context.

Finish your essay in style

You could say:

> In conclusion, Dickens uses language and contrast to present family as important, because of the companionship, happiness and support it brings.

1) This conclusion is okay but it doesn't summarise the whole of the essay very well.

2) So to make it really impressive you could say something like...

> 'A Christmas Carol' portrays family relationships as an important aspect of a good and happy life. Dickens uses examples of happy family relationships, such as the Cratchits, Belle's family and Fan's relationship with Scrooge, to present families as an important source of happiness and support. Scrooge's solitary life is a stark contrast to this; the comparison of his life to the happy families in the novel strongly emphasises how much joy and comfort being in a family can bring.

Make your last sentence really stand out — it's your last opportunity to impress the examiner.

Why do alligators write good essays — their quotes are so snappy...

It seems like there's a lot to remember on these two pages, but there's not really. To summarise — write a scorching intro and a sizzling conclusion, make a good range of points (one per paragraph) and include plenty of examples. Easy.

Index

Index

Charles Dickens's 'A Christmas Carol'

The Characters in 'A Christmas Carol'

Phew! You should be an expert on *A Christmas Carol* by now. But if you want a bit of light relief and a quick recap of the novel's plot, sit yourself down and read through *A Christmas Carol — The Cartoon...*

Ebenezer
Scrooge

As a child

As a young man

Marley's
Ghost

Bob
Cratchit

Tiny Tim

Fred

Ghost of
Christmas Past

Ghost of Christmas
Yet to Come

Ghost of Christmas Present

Charles Dickens's 'A Christmas Carol'